"The compassion and openhearted learning on display here will stay with you for a long time, and remind you of just how transformative close friendships can be."

—**Heather Havrilesky, author of**
How to Be a Person in the World

"Joyous, vulnerable, honest, and moving."

—**J. Ryan Stradal, author of**
Kitchens of the Great Midwest **and**
The Lager Queen of Minnesota

"[A] thoughtful and highly readable story . . . Friendship is a choice. With this book, Sow and Friedman remind us that laziness in tending to friendships is dangerous, and that regardless of the circumstance, whether geography or pandemic, friendships must be nourished, or they will wither."

—*The New York Times Book Review*

"Big Friendship is an anatomy of the way one particular friendship works, but it is also an argument for taking all amicable relationships more seriously, for understanding them in the terms we usually reserve for romance (the authors share their "meet cute" and discuss the "spark" and "chemistry" between them), and for appreciating the sometimes difficult and time-consuming work it takes to maintain these friendships."

—*Vogue*

"Brilliant and honest."

—**Katie Couric**

"A cozy, earnest read . . . *Big Friendship* is unfailingly warm. Writing with the crystalline hindsight of friends who learned the hard way, Sow and Friedman reveal the hidden origins of the schisms they paid good money for a therapist to help them heal. After reading this book, their readers might not have to."

—*Slate*

"A deeply funny and immensely heartfelt look into what makes a friendship last despite time, distance, trials, and major life changes."

—*Elle*

"In sharing their personal story, alongside research from social scientists, Sow and Friedman highlight what it takes for a friendship to last."

—*Time* **magazine**

"In *Big Friendship*, Aminatou Sow and Ann Friedman save their friendship—and maybe even yours."

—**SHONDALAND**

Simon & Schuster Paperbacks

New York   London   Toronto   Sydney   New Delhi

BIG FRIENDSHIP
HOW WE KEEP EACH OTHER CLOSE

AMINATOU SOW

ANN FRIEDMAN

Simon & Schuster Paperbacks
An Imprint of Simon & Schuster, Inc.
1230 Avenue of the Americas
New York, NY 10020

First Simon & Schuster trade paperback edition July 2021

SIMON & SCHUSTER PAPERBACKS and colophon are registered
trademarks of Simon & Schuster, Inc.

For information about special discounts for bulk purchases,
please contact Simon & Schuster Special Sales at
1-866-506-1949 or business@simonandschuster.com.

The Simon & Schuster Speakers Bureau can bring authors to
your live event. For more information or to book an event, contact
the Simon & Schuster Speakers Bureau at 1-866-248-3049 or
visit our website at www.simonspeakers.com.

Cover design by Elizabeth Spiridakis Olson
Interior design by Lewelin Polanco

Manufactured in the United States of America

1   3   5   7   9   10   8   6   4   2

Library of Congress Cataloging-in-Publication Data

Names: Sow, Aminatou, author. | Friedman, Ann, author.
Title: Big friendship : how we keep each other close /
Aminatou Sow and Ann Friedman.
Description: New York : Simon & Schuster, 2020. |
Summary: "Two of the nation's leading feminists and hosts of the
hit podcast "Call Your Girlfriend" make the bold and compelling
argument that a close friendship is the most influential and
important relationship a human life can contain—helping
you improve as a person and in your relationships
with others" —Provided by publisher.
Identifiers: LCCN 2020002283 | ISBN 9781982111908
(hardcover) | ISBN 9781982111922 (ebook)
Subjects: LCSH: Female friendship. | Interpersonal relations.
Classification: LCC BF575.F66 S627 2020 | DDC 177/.62082—dc23
LC record available at https://lccn.loc.gov/2020002283

ISBN 978-1-9821-1190-8
ISBN 978-1-9821-1191-5 (pbk)
ISBN 978-1-9821-1192-2 (ebook)

FOR AMINA.
Thank you for risking yourself
for me again and again.

FOR ANN.
You are worth it. I hope we find
each other in every lifetime.

BIG FRIENDSHIP is a bond of great strength, force, and significance that transcends life phases, geography, and emotional shifts. It is large in dimension, affecting most aspects of each person's life. It is full of meaning and resonance. A Big Friendship is reciprocal, with both parties feeling worthy of each other and willing to give of themselves in generous ways. A Big Friendship is active. Hearty. And almost always, a Big Friendship is mature. Its advanced age commands respect and predicts its ability to last far into the future.

Contents

Prologue   xiii

ONE   The Spark   1

TWO   Obsessed   21

THREE   Chosen Family   45

FOUR   I Don't Shine If You Don't Shine   59

FIVE   The Stretch   83

SIX   The Friendweb   99

SEVEN   The Trapdoor   117

EIGHT   See You on the Internet   139

NINE   Too Big to Fail   163

TEN   The Long Haul   187

Acknowledgments   207
Notes   213

Prologue

It should have been a perfect weekend. The entrance to the spa was a white mission-style building with a wide arched doorway and the words "Natural Baths" in relief above. Beyond it was the real draw, an Olympic-size mineral pool with licks of steam slowly peeling off it. The scene was ringed with hills and palms. And as the Northern California sun dipped behind the pines, there we were: two women sitting on parallel beds in one of the picture-perfect cottages on the property. We were each wrapped in a fluffy white bathrobe. Ann was on the phone ordering a pizza and a Caesar salad, and Aminatou was deciding what movie to watch. The only thing on the schedule for the next 48 hours was a series of side-by-side spa treatments—with plenty of time for floating in the pool.

The emails we sent in advance of the trip were all exclamation points and promises. "Totes getting a mud bath but feeling conflicted about body scrub. Maybe a facial??" "Oooh, the mud bath is included!" "Y E S to free mud bath! and to this lil getaway." Once we arrived, we texted cheerful updates to mutual friends who weren't on the trip: "Hi from the spa in Napa!" On social media we posted cute photos of our matching animal-print shoes and beautiful scenes of the sun glinting on the surface of that 92-degrees natural hot-spring pool.

By all outward appearances, we were two healthy, wealthy women on a gorgeous getaway. This was the stuff of stereotypical "girls' trips," the sort of extravagant vacation we had dreamed about taking when we first met as broke 20-somethings. Years deep into our friendship, with so many of our professional aspirations starting to come to fruition and big pieces of our lives starting to snap into place, our unhurried hours at the spa should have been every bit as idyllic as the photos made it out to be.

But we were miserable.

We were miserable in that pretending-you-aren't-miserable way, lonely behind our respective emotional walls. Just a few hours in, the trip was feeling like an awkward family reunion or a sad couples retreat, the sort of trying-too-hard getaway designed to revive a fading relationship. We were not a romantic couple or estranged family members, but the stakes were just as high for us.

We had met five years earlier and had quickly become essential in each other's lives. You know that clip of Oprah talking about Gayle? ("She is the mother I never had. She is the sister everybody would want. She is the friend that everybody deserves. I don't know a better person.") That was the level of teary-eyed appreciation we had for each other. We knew each other's secrets and snack preferences as if they were our own. Most of our friends considered us an inseparable duo. We had also started a podcast together, so lots of strangers now thought of us that way too. In the past, nothing about our friendship felt forced. We loved being—and being known as—each other's core person. But over the last year, a space had opened up between us. This trip was an acknowledgment that our friendship was failing. We hoped that some bonding time and superficial luxuries just might save it.

The next day at brunch, we struggled to find things to say. We had quickly agreed to stay in and watch a movie the night before because it meant a few hours when we didn't have to carefully choose which anecdotes to share about our lives as we avoided topics that felt too loaded. But now here we were in the light of day, sitting across from each other. We talked about the weather. The food. The baby-smooth quality of our post-spa skin. The banter felt forced, and we both knew we weren't comfortable enough for deeper topics.

Later, when it came time for our free mud baths, we were shy about disrobing in front of each other. *This* was a first. We'd been in spa settings and in thrift-store changing rooms together countless times. As we sank into our respective tubs, Aminatou exhaled in relaxation. Then she glanced over and noticed that Ann was struggling with the heat. (Ann is basically a lizard. She's always either freezing or boiling.) Aminatou, a more experienced spa-goer, realized she had forgotten to warn Ann that the mud bath feels very hot and claustrophobic. Aminatou hadn't done it on purpose, but she was convinced that in an earlier, better time in the friendship, she would have remembered to check in with Ann about this. Suddenly Aminatou was not so relaxed either.

Prologue

It felt like a metaphor for our dysfunctional dynamic.

At dinner that night, we acknowledged that things between us had gotten bad and that we wanted them to be better. There were long, uncomfortable pauses. Usually our conversations relied on us knowing everything about each other, and we had stopped offering up those details many months ago. Ann didn't get into her financial woes or the knot of feelings she had about moving in with her formerly long-distance boyfriend. It wasn't until the ride back to the city that Aminatou mentioned to Ann that she had been dating someone she really liked—for *months*. This was the first time Ann was hearing his name.

On the ride home, we told ourselves that things felt better than they had before. That this was progress, the beginning of a return to the time when our friendship felt like steady breathing, both natural and crucial, important and on autopilot. *At least we admitted to each other that our friendship needs work*, we both thought. *It's a start.* We didn't say these things out loud, though. Lodged beneath our rib cages was the truth: We had both been dreading this trip because we suspected a beautiful, distraction-free setting would highlight just how wide the space between us had become. And we had been right.

We didn't have the words for what was happening to us or what had happened to our friendship.

If you listen to our podcast, you are probably screaming right now. Not only because we are women who seem to have a *lot* of words for everything else but also because our show is premised on us being tight-knit besties. (Stay sexy and don't fake your friendship to keep your podcast afloat!) You might feel like we played you. But the truth is, like any long-term intimate relationship, a friendship like ours is complicated. It's far more accurate to say we played ourselves by spending so many months pretending that things were OK when clearly they were not.

This isn't the only time we have lacked a vocabulary for the dynamics and milestones and ups and downs of our relationship. In the past, when the world failed to provide a label for something we were experiencing as friends, we often supplied our own words for it. We came up with our own shorthand for the powerful decision to invest in our friends the way we invest in ourselves. (It's called Shine Theory! Such a great concept that everyone from Victoria's Secret to Reese Witherspoon has tried to co-opt it.) We talk about our messy, beautiful, interconnected social groups as a "friendweb." The good stuff? We have always been adept at finding ways of describing it.

But it has been much harder for us to find a language for the difficult parts: The frustration of giving more to a friend than they're giving back. The unbridgeable gaps in even the closest of interracial friendships. The dynamic of pushing each other away even as we're trying to reconnect. The struggle to find true peace with a long-term friendship that is changing. We even lacked a name for the *kind* of friendship we have. Words like "best friend" or "BFF" don't capture the adult emotional work we've put into this relationship.

We now call it a Big Friendship, because it's one of the most affirming—and most complicated—relationships that a human life can hold.

We would love to tell you that after we returned home from our sad spa weekend we quickly patched things up and got on with our legendary friendship. But the truth is, it took a really long time and a lot of false starts. Five years later, we are still figuring out how to stay centered in each other's lives. We are still searching for the right words. And honestly, we have a lot of compassion for our past selves, stewing in those separate mud baths. We understand why it was so hard for us to figure out what was happening to us. At a cultural level, there is a lot of lip service about friendship being wonderful and important, but not a lot of social support for protecting what's precious about it. Even deep, lasting friendships like ours need protection—and, sometimes, repair.

So how did we go from being the most important people in each other's lives to near strangers and back again? And why would *anyone* put themselves through the torture of trying to stay in a complicated friendship for the long haul?

That's the story we are about to tell you.

We are telling it with one voice, and in one narrative thread, because we want you to always feel secure that, hey, we are *still friends*. (And we are!) Figuring out how to share our story in a "we" voice also helped us find the overlap in our experiences. There are, of course, some clear differences between us, and places where our stories diverge. So in these places, we refer to ourselves as "Aminatou" and "Ann" separately.

We are not sharing our story because we think it's exceptional. Quite the opposite. We've spent so much time examining our friendship because we believe many of its joys and pitfalls are pretty common. We hope that you won't think of us as experts (you'll soon find out why we aren't), but rather as two people who love each other very much. Two friends who, 10 years in, are still finding so much delight and mystery at the heart of their relationship. Who are searching together for the words to describe both the expansive possibilities and the painful challenges of friend-ship. Who are obsessing over the question of how to stay in each other's lives forever.

We have been enlightened and humbled to tell this story to each other. And now we are honored to tell it to you.

ONE

..

The Spark

L ike any great American love story, ours began at prom. OK, actually, it was the prom episode of *Gossip Girl*. In 2009, like all pop-culture obsessives, we were dedicated viewers of this trashy teen soap opera set in the world of wealthy Manhattan private schools. Our mutual friend Dayo decided to host a viewing party, and we were both invited to watch the melodramatic scenes unfold from a semicircle of ratty couches in the old DC row house where she lived with several roommates.

Aminatou recognized a few names on the email invitation but had never met any of the other guests. It felt a little intimidating to meet up with this already-established group, but she knew that if she was going to make new friends, she had to get out of the house and be proactive about showing up to things. And she had the perfect thing to wear: a T-shirt that said "CHUCK+BLAIR," the brattiest teen couple on the show. Her college bestie Brittany had made it for her.

That night Ann noticed Aminatou's shirt right away and was impressed by her level of dedication to the party theme. As Ann sipped her manhattan—a nod to the show's setting and a deliberately "chic" cocktail chosen by Dayo to match the *Gossip Girl* aesthetic—she noted that the snappiest rejoinders to the on-screen action seemed to be coming from Aminatou. Ann was used to spending time with people who had jobs at the intersection of media and politics, so the commentary and banter always flowed easily in her friend group. But that night Ann hung on to Amina-tou's every word and laughed extra hard at all of her jokes.

"How did you two meet?" When we find ourselves at a party, our favorite ice breaker is asking a pair of friends how they know each other. Romantic couples are probably asked this question most often. But friendship origin stories are no less powerful. A look of excitement crosses friends' faces when they're especially pleased with their own version of events. And even if they're reluctant to open up, with a little prodding people will usually confess what they thought of the other person before befriending them. We love the accounts jointly told by friends who finish each other's sentences or fill in the blanks, trading off as they tell their familiar story at a rapid-fire clip. And we love it almost as much when it's clear the friends have never been asked to reflect on this, and we get to hear their story as they're telling it for the first time.

We can learn so much about someone by the way they talk about their friends. And we can learn a lot about a friendship from a joint recounting of its beginning. Are they brand-new friends who are obsessed with each other right now? Have they known each other for decades? Did they used to be lovers? Is there some unevenness to their narratives, as if one person is more invested than the other? It's all revealed in the telling of their story.

We have told our own origin story dozens of times, and we often talk about our meet-cute like it was dumb luck. But the truth is, it may have been inevitable. Aminatou's apartment was a 15-minute walk away from Ann's. We worked a few blocks apart too. Although there is a three-year age gap between us, we were both in our mid-20s and moved in overlapping social circles. We were at the same party on the same night because we had a lot of people in common—including our friend Dayo.

Ann had been introduced to Dayo the previous year and quickly noticed her declarative opinions, easy laugh, and gorgeous handbag. It seems stupid to mention the handbag, but among her peers—all underpaid political journalists—there were only canvas tote bags and backpacks. *No one* had a nice leather bag. Wherever this woman was going, Ann wanted to tag along. She and Dayo soon saw each other regularly at group dinners and TV viewing nights, when they piled into the living room of a friend who had cable. Dayo was a small-talk queen with irrepressible energy who somehow managed to turn boring "How's work going?" questions into intense philosophical debates. Often, before what would invariably turn out to be a disappointing house party on a Saturday night, Ann would head to Dayo's early and arrange herself on top of a pile of rejected outfits, sipping a whiskey while Dayo finished getting dressed. "There's no skirt too short if you're wearing tights," Dayo once trilled, slipping into a miniskirt in the depths of winter. With Dayo, Ann always felt like she should be taking notes, recording the hilarious aphorisms that dropped from her mouth.

Meanwhile, Aminatou knew Dayo from work. Or rather, she knew *of* Dayo. Aminatou was on staff at a think tank, often at the front desk greeting visitors, and Dayo had a fellowship there, which meant she dropped by the office only every so often. They hadn't crossed paths yet, but Aminatou had been called "Dayo" more than once. Aminatou was annoyed at the mistake, but she was dying to meet the mysterious other Black woman with the Nigerian name. When they finally got together, over bowls of ramen, they shared a knowing laugh about the doppelgänger situation—they looked nothing alike. They debated African diaspora issues. They realized they were into the same foreign movies and music. Clearly, this was going somewhere.

Oh my god, you need to meet my friend Ann, Dayo thought. A few weeks later, she sent Ann a message about organizing a *Gossip Girl* viewing party.

DAYO: I really really like this girl aminatou
ANN: i'm excited to meet aminatou sow. That girl knows like everyone i know, yet i haven't met her
DAYO: oh she's excellent. what's the drills with gossip girl? she's a big fan

A plan was hatched: Dayo would host and invite Aminatou. "I want to say that there is an element of 'Oh, how nice that everything worked out,'" Dayo told us many years later. "But thinking through this now, there was a lot more intention to it." She knew before we did that we needed to be in each other's lives.

It's hard to remember who we were that night at Dayo's house, before we were friends. Not only because it was a long time ago,

4

but also because we have changed each other in countless ways, from the profound to the imperceptible. We didn't just meet each other that night. We began the process of making each other into the people we are today. Although we're self-confident enough to know that we would have been great if our paths had never converged, we cannot imagine what that alternate reality looks like. It's impossible to untangle us.

This feeling of being inextricable is a hallmark of Big Friendship. As humans, we are all thoroughly shaped by the people we know and love. Day to day, our friends influence our tastes and our moods. Long term, they can also affect how we feel about our bodies, how we spend our money, and the political views we hold. We grow in response to each other, in ways both intentional and subconscious.

Behind every meet-cute is an emotional origin story, one that answers a deeper question. Not "How did you two meet?" but "Why did you become so deeply embedded in each other's lives?"

"We met at a friend's house" is the superficial narrative we tell to strangers. But our real origin story is that we met at a time in our lives when we were both a little bit lost. We were both figuring out how to set a course for where we were hoping to go. And in each other, we found someone who already understood who we wanted to be.

Four years before she met Aminatou, Ann was arriving in San Francisco for her first-ever magazine job. It was a short-term fact-checking gig at a lefty publication known for its investigative reporting. (Basically, an internship that paid a small stipend, which Ann supplemented with the savings she'd built up the previous year, working a nonjournalism job.) Immediately, she felt sure that she was in the right place. She loved sitting at the edges of the conference room, listening to the editors at the table debate which topics were worthy of the magazine and make the case for stories they wanted to commission. She befriended a few of her fellow fact-checkers, as well as several women who worked in the fundraising and marketing departments, and they'd go out drinking and dancing together. She even fell in love with one of the journalists at work, and they started dating. Ann and her boyfriend spent weekends making pizza from scratch and taking day trips up Highway 1. Often at night she walked the city's roller-coaster hills home to the small room she was subletting in a Victorian near Alamo Square Park, drunk on whiskey gingers and the feeling that she was shaping her life into something she loved. But she knew it couldn't last—she was surviving on canned beans and unsure of her next professional step. San Francisco sparkled with a just-out-of-reach charm.

As this glorified internship was coming to an end, Ann managed to score a coffee meeting about a full-time position at an online magazine in the Bay Area. This felt like a minor miracle, as California had precious few media jobs. She had heard whispers from a few young women that this potential new boss was a monster, but she was in no position to turn down opportunities. When she showed up to the coffee shop, the boss confirmed the rumors by immediately making a bizarre comment about her body. ("Mmmmm . . . really tall women like big sunglasses, huh?") The meeting was so casual that Ann didn't even realize it had been a job interview until the offer arrived. But she ignored the neon sign flashing "This Is Going to Be Awful." She quickly accepted because the annual salary was more than she could comprehend—$40,000—and it was a big professional step up: she would be writing headlines and editing short articles. How bad could this boss really be?

Pro tip: if you are creeped out at a meeting so informal you don't realize it's a job interview, *run*.

It was worse than Ann imagined to work for a lecherous bully. At her one-month performance review, the boss demanded to know why she refused to discuss her personal life with him and said, in an unmistakably threatening tone, "You know, most new employees try to *please* the boss." (He got his comeuppance many years later, when an entire episode of the radio show *This American Life* was dedicated to his misbehavior.) Ann couldn't imagine working for him much longer but didn't know where else she'd even apply.

Then Ann's boyfriend moved to Washington, DC, to start a prestigious but underpaid gig at a political magazine. From a different sublet in a different Victorian (Ann moved three times that year), she talked to him with her phone pressed against a window because her bedroom was a cell-reception dead zone. He relayed the conversations and inside jokes he had with a new crew of friends, who were all young journalists. Ann had to force herself to laugh along.

As she searched for a new job in San Francisco, her boyfriend stepped in with a plan. He was about to turn down an entry-level editing job he had been recruited for at a different DC magazine, and he could put forward Ann's name for the position. In some ways, this came as a relief to her: job hunting in California was a nightmare. She also missed being in the same zip code as her boyfriend. And if she was honest, she was hungry to prove herself professionally.

At the same time, Ann worried that she didn't know enough about policy to hack it in the world of political journalism and that this magazine would be interviewing her only as a courtesy to her boyfriend. (Her ego still feels tender just thinking about it.) If she got the job, it would mean taking an almost $10,000 pay cut. And then there was her deep sadness at the thought of saying goodbye to California and her friends there, who had become dear to her so quickly. But she decided there was no harm in applying. When she got the job, it just made sense to say yes. She hated that this life decision could be headlined "How My Boyfriend Got Me a Job and I Left My Friends to Be with Him." She put in two weeks' notice with the bullying boss, who slammed his office door in her face, and she assured her California friends that she was going to DC for only a year, tops. This is not how careers work! But this is the only way Ann could convince herself to move.

As Ann drove eastward across the country, her dented green Honda was heavy with her every earthly possession and a growing sense of dread. She had repeatedly tried and failed to argue herself out of this move. Professionally, she was sure it was a good choice. She was also certain it was the right thing for her long-distance relationship. It made sense in every way, except for the fact that she didn't really want to live in a swamp full of status-obsessed former debate champions. Ann, who had always followed politics and was on her own high-school debate team for a few years, considered herself *above* DC before she even arrived. Moving was her choice, but it was one she made reluctantly. And so she showed up with the pouty energy of a preschooler being sent to time-out: compliant but with an air of superiority.

At Ann's new job, the magazine's founders and top-level

editors were older men who were eager to heap praise and opportunities on her male colleagues. She felt like she had to fight to be heard. Several nights a week, the 20-somethings in the office (plus, occasionally, an older male editor) would head to a dive bar across the street for happy-hour beers and chicken tenders. It felt to Ann like an extension of the office, not a decompression from it. It was her choice to attend, but these nights left her exhausted and, often, lonely. Still, it was easier to blame her workplace, the city itself, anything but her own shitty attitude about this life transition. She wrote to one of her college besties: "I'm uneasy, and wondering if this fast-track journalism thing is right for me (and if it isn't, what is?). I'm starting to think I need to avoid the east coast altogether." How was it possible that her career felt like it was moving too fast *and* too slow at the same time?

But she was grateful to have a job at all, given the apocalyptic predictions for her industry. Ann stuck it out, working her way up to editing long articles for the print magazine—which was a minor miracle given that the country was in the midst of a historic recession. She spent her days holding her nose while editing opinion pieces about how this economic collapse was actually a "once-in-a-lifetime policy opportunity." Ann found solace in her side hustle, contributing to a feminist blog, where she seethed about the wage gap and wondered whether the Pope might enjoy invasive regulation of *his* body. She also spent a lot of time clicking through a folder of California photos she kept on her work computer.

The job never stopped feeling like an uneasy fit. But Ann had coworkers she really liked and respected. A few years in, she had learned to draw better boundaries, avoiding the after-work events that often turned into beer-fueled political debates. She moved with her boyfriend into a small one-bedroom apartment, which was pretty cozy despite its dingy wall-to-wall carpeting and the sickening ginkgo smell that wafted in through the windows every fall.

Now that she wasn't brand-new to the city, Ann had also made a few excellent friends outside her work world who were eager to join her in the crowd at music shows and on thrift-shopping excursions to the Virginia suburbs, which were a gold mine for vintage silks and leather skirts. A few people, like Dayo, had crossed over from professional acquaintances to true friends. And one of Ann's college besties, Lara, had even moved to town. Lara had a relentlessly curious nature that helped Ann start to readjust her own perspective on DC. Lara never wanted to talk about work, loved to dance, and was a reliable museum-going buddy. And, best of all, she lived close enough that one day when Ann locked herself out of her apartment with no shoes on, she walked to Lara's place in her socks.

So as Ann messaged Dayo about planning a *Gossip Girl* viewing night, things were better than when she had first landed in town three years earlier. But she still missed her friends back in San Francisco, and she had a feeling of impending abandonment: Lara was on the verge of quitting her job and leaving town. Sure, DC was where Ann lived, but it didn't feel like home. In a way, it never would. Her fond memories are not of walking its wide diagonal avenues or gazing out the window of her office or even sweaty dance nights at the Black Cat. Her attachment to the city is defined by the people she met there. One person in particular.

The Spark

Two years before she met Ann, Aminatou arrived in DC as an international student freshly graduated from the University of Texas, with big dreams and enough money to cover a month of rent and a few cheap beers. On the day of her commencement ceremony, a friend had remarked, "Something weird is happening with the economy. People usually have jobs lined up before graduation." But Aminatou wasn't too worried that she didn't have a single job prospect. The plan all along had been to move to DC with or without one. Aminatou had always thought she would follow in her father's footsteps and work in international policy. She had studied political science and Middle Eastern studies in college, and she liked that DC felt like an international city. She had always felt drawn to its architecture because it was the one American city that looked like it was built by 19th-century Europeans. Aminatou had fallen in love with the idea of living there during a solo high-school trip and made herself a promise to come back as an adult.

She quickly found a place in a group house in Dupont Circle, a picturesque neighborhood in Northwest DC filled with beautiful embassies. She moved into a tiny room in the charming yellow row house. She was adamant about sleeping on a queen-size bed, which took up the entire room, leaving just enough space to prop up a full-length mirror. Priorities! She used every inch of wall space, including above the bed, for bookshelves. Her roommates were already very good friends with each other, and Aminatou was definitely the Third Roommate. They often went out to bars and the occasional dinner, but Aminatou didn't feel close to them. She knew only a few people in DC: some girls from college and a boy who had been ahead of her in boarding school who now worked for a cartoonishly evil congressman. Aminatou couldn't quite understand why something that had never been difficult for her before—fitting in—seemed impossible now. But she would worry about her social life later. First, she was preoccupied with finding a job.

Her college friend had been right: the economy was definitely weird. Aminatou fired off hundreds, truly hundreds, of job queries. She was offered an internship in Senator John Kerry's office, but she had to turn it down when she found out it was unpaid. "How is everyone else supporting themselves while interning full-time?" she asked herself over and over again.

Her job search was more urgent than most. Aminatou had moved to the United States on a student visa at the start of her college years, and now that she had graduated she would soon need an employer to sponsor her to stay in the country. International students are eligible for a 12-month work authorization called Optional Practical Training that starts as soon as their paperwork is approved. To stay in the country beyond that, Aminatou would need an H-1B work visa. This meant racing the immigration clock to find an employer that could be convinced to hire her and then petition the government to keep her around. A tall order, especially when most Americans don't understand their own immigration laws.

If Aminatou was lucky enough to get an interview, the visa issue became a barrier. It slowly dawned on her that her hustle wasn't the problem. She had moved to a city built on money and connections, and she had neither.

She wasn't defeated, though. She got a seasonal job at a bougie toy store—which wouldn't solve the visa issue but would at least pay her rent. This was at the height of a Chinese lead-paint toy recall, and American parents were wary of anything with a "Made in China" sticker. The owner of the toy store imported all the minimalist wooden French toys Aminatou had grown up with and added some extra zeros to the price tag. A wonderful scam.

Days at the toy store were boring. She couldn't (and still cannot) wrap gifts to save her life, and the customers could be so condescending. The job paid the bills, but Aminatou often walked the 1.8 miles to work when she couldn't afford to take the bus. She was worried, but she kept applying for other positions, optimistic that she might just get lucky.

Almost halfway through her 12-month work authorization, she got hired for a decidedly nonglitzy admin position at a think tank. The salary was listed at $28,000 per year and she was proud of herself when she negotiated them up to $32,000—just enough to pay rent and bills and buy a bottle of tequila at the end of the week. She walked to work, past manicured parks and beautiful embassies. She felt rich! Aminatou figured she would work her way from the front desk into a policy position—which they had assured her was a possibility—and launch her career from there. (You will be unsurprised to learn that this global domination plan hatched by a wide-eyed millennial did not pan out.)

Her responsibilities were mostly sending mail and entering data, and she was frustrated that no matter who she asked, they had nothing substantive for her to do. Working at the front desk also meant that people always tried to dump their errands and menial tasks on her. She refused, and reminded them that fetching coffee wasn't her job. The colleagues who were closest to her in age all seemed to have decided that she wasn't one of them, and they made it a point to "forget" to invite her to happy hours. She didn't mind, though. They were all boring, and having boundaries between her work and personal lives seemed like a good idea.

Until she met Cecille.

Even though Aminatou worked at one of the "sexier" think tanks in town, it was still an endless parade of men in ill-fitting suits and women in sweater sets. The fashion wasn't the real issue, though. DC had plenty of fun and interesting people who dressed very well. Aminatou just hadn't found anyone at work who would laugh at her jokes about how current financial regulations mirrored trends in indie music. That is, until she ran into a woman with a pink rattail in the copy room. Aminatou was hooked the instant Cecille described her own look as "Sarajevo chic." They became inseparable, called each other "boo boo," and created the first culturally relevant policy nerd blog, Orszagasm.com. Yes, an entire blog dedicated to the hunky Peter Orszag, the 2009–2010 director of the Office of Management and Budget. Tag line: "Putting the OMG back in the OMB."

Cecille was frighteningly smart and equally hilarious. She got it. She never made Aminatou feel bad about being broke or working at the front desk. After knowing each other for less than a year, they moved in together. (U-Haul lesbian stereotypes have nothing on Cecille and Aminatou's friendship. When you know, you know, OK?) Cecille didn't have an impressive salary either, but they pooled their money to live a lifestyle they found comfortable. Years later, they took pride in saying, "We were very broke but we always had cable!" (Note: This is terrible, terrible personal finance in action! Cut the cable and eat real food instead of splitting Five Guys fries for lunch every day.)

They had a group of friends they hung out with fairly consistently. Aminatou sent out regular emails inviting everyone to shenanigans most Thursdays through Sundays. (Monday through Wednesday was for nursing hangovers and resting.) They had a lot of fun sneaking in their own alcohol to Jazz in the Garden at the National Gallery, exploring the monuments at night, and seeing pretty much every band that played the 9:30 Club. Aminatou and Cecille almost always arrived and left together. They were a unit. They had bonded very quickly because neither of them was connecting with DC in a forever kind of way, so Aminatou braced herself for the day Cecille would tell her she was leaving town. Aminatou channeled that anxiety into meeting new people.

And so, when she opened the email invitation to watch *Gossip Girl* at Dayo's house, she immediately replied that she would go.

She landed on the couch next to Ann.

W e got lucky. We had both made our way to the same city, within a few years of each other. The scene was set.

It's no coincidence that we met in what was still technically prime time for friend making: our 20s. Up to that point, most of our friendships had been created within the bounds of institutions—families, school, work—which honestly had turned out great for us. (Of course this isn't true for everyone. Some people struggle as children and teenagers; others have strict rules against making friends at work.) But we both yearned to meet friends we hadn't always been stuck in the same boat with. Separately, and at a deep level, we were both looking to establish our own village on the shore.

There's a popular belief that people age out of this desire to make friends. They get married or have kids or get a demanding job, and see their free time shrink. They make a choice to focus on the people they already know rather than trying to meet new friends. But even on the other side of a big life event, people can find themselves looking around and wishing they had more friendships rooted in deep connection.

And in our experience, periods of transition—at any age— have been opportunities to make friends. We've each tended to form our deepest new bonds after we've made a change in our lives: switching jobs, ending a romantic relationship, moving to a new city. Looking to befriend people who are also searching for something has always panned out better for us than trying to wedge our way into an existing tight-knit group or onto the calendar of someone with long-established social ties in the area. At the time we met, we shared a general restlessness, a fear of losing a close friend who was threatening to move away, and a deep uncertainty about the future.

Of course, sometimes we've fallen so hard for a new friend that space and time and circumstances aren't huge factors. We've found room in our schedules (and in our hearts—*awwww*) that we didn't know was there, usually because we had so much chemistry.

We're talking about an initial *ZING!* feeling. It can't be forced, and that's why it's so magical. You can work alongside someone for years, or be their classmate all the way through school, or always be happy to bump into them at a party, but if you don't have that je ne sais quoi, it's not going to lead anywhere.

With each other, we felt a spark right away. Ann was instantly

16

taken with Aminatou's combination of worldliness and easy approachability. Aminatou could sense that Ann was whip smart and worked hard—two of the sexiest friend qualities, to be honest. When Aminatou told Ann about Orszagasm, Ann howled. We could tell we were both nerds, but the shared pop-culture references and the aesthetic sensibility were there too.

This spark didn't carry any romantic or sexual implications for either of us. What we felt was platonic, but exciting nonetheless. Even our brief interaction at a TV party hinted at a certain easy rapport. We wanted to know more. We wanted to impress each other. It was a powerful attraction.

"All the research on attraction can usually be applied to friendship as well," says Emily Langan, a communications professor at Wheaton College who studies all kinds of close relationships. "It's attractiveness in style. It's attractiveness in aesthetics, sort of the vibe they give off. It's attractiveness in personality as well." Much of this, she notes, happens at a subconscious level. It's often hard to articulate exactly *why* you're attracted to someone. You just are. And sometimes it's even hard to say how you want that attraction to manifest. Do you want to be this person's lover? Their best friend? Their spouse? Their creative collaborator?

At the sparking point of many relationships, it's not always clear. And it's common for two people to interpret the spark in different ways, with one reading it as platonic while the other experiences it as romantic or as something else altogether. Many of us jump to quickly define the feeling based on context. If the other person is of a compatible sexuality, we might interpret the spark as sexual. If we meet them in a professional context, we might think of them as a potential collaborator. If we are in a monogamous romantic relationship, we might choose to read all fresh sparks as platonic.

The same combination of emotions can be categorized many ways, from platonic to romantic to something else altogether, writes Angela Chen in her book *Ace: What Asexuality Reveals About Desire, Society, and the Meaning of Sex*. For Chen, who identifies as asexual and therefore doesn't use "I want to have sex with them or not" as the primary way of sorting brand-new relationships into platonic/romantic categories, the spark feeling carries a sense of undefined possibility. "When I first meet someone, I don't know whether we're aligned on what we want," she told us in an interview. "And I think that's what makes it both exciting and confusing for me. The uncertainty of not only 'Will they like me?' but 'Will they like me in the exact same way that I want?' Like, will we align?" This is something most of us feel at a moment of spark: we want this other person to like us back in the same way and the same amount that we like them, even if we haven't fully defined those terms to ourselves yet. And we are excited to find out whether that happens.

In our case, it was a good match. Of course, this was not something explicitly hashed out in our first conversation. In the days and weeks following the moment of spark, we both settled into the knowledge that we were aligned, and we've been aligned ever since. It's worth noting that what people want from a relationship can evolve over time, past the moment of spark. One or both parties can decide they feel more romantic or sexual about it—or less. This is how you get friends who used to be lovers, and lovers who used to be friends. This is how you get a person who claims they're being "friendzoned" by someone who's always been strictly interested in the platonic. The lines aren't as brightly drawn for everyone as they've been in our particular friendship.

Even in an unambiguous friendship like ours, the first whirlwind moments can feel a lot like falling in love. In the heady weeks after we met, we weren't trying to get in each other's pants, but rather in each other's brains. In the eyes of the other, we each had an undefinable emotional appeal that was at once adventurous, mysterious, and idealized. In other words, it was exciting in that pit-of-the-stomach way. This kind of immediate connection is rare, so when it happens it's incredible—as in *not credible*, as in so magical it's difficult to believe.

What made our initial bond special is that it felt effortless. We had each been in social settings where small talk felt like hard labor and none of our jokes seemed to land. This dynamic between us, by contrast, didn't feel like work at all. Sure, we were probably trying to impress each other a little—OK, a lot. But mostly it felt like our meet-cute happened *to* us. Like we didn't even have a say in the matter.

If you'd asked us about friendship on that first night, we would have told you we were pretty good at it already. We figured that we knew how to hold on to the great friends we had while also making new ones . . . and that, with minimal effort, we would keep all of these important people around until our blissful *Golden Girls*–style group retirement situation. We thought we'd simply have solid friendships for life. Just set it and forget it. See you on the lanai.

But deep down, we also knew that we could let our friendships slide in order to bolster the other areas of our lives. Friends are expected to be forgiving of this kind of neglect. Trying to get that promotion? You gotta put in long hours and can't hang out after work. Just met someone you might want to spend your life with romantically? It's OK, your friends will understand why you had to cancel on them.

At this stage in our lives, we had a lot of time for our friends, so it wasn't important to examine exactly where they fell on our priorities list. They were at the top by default, and we figured they'd stay there. We had never considered that we'd find the rough patches of our friendships to be more difficult than any career roadblock and more painful than the worst romantic breakup. Given what we were about to go through over the next decade, our idea of friendship as a respite from the "actual hard stuff" of life is downright laughable. We had no idea what we were in for.

We were just excited to have met each other.

The credits rolled on the *Gossip Girl* episode, and a heavy spring rain started to fall outside Dayo's row house. As Aminatou walked down the front steps and opened her umbrella, she hoped Ann would be headed in the same direction. But Ann went the opposite way. Aminatou waved goodbye, maybe a little too enthusiastically. There were no phone numbers exchanged, no promises to find each other on social media, not even a "hope to see you around."

Aminatou shouldn't have worried, though. By the time she got home and logged on to Facebook to find Ann, she already had a friend request waiting.

And of course she clicked "Accept."

TWO

..

Obsessed

The very next night, Ann had plans to attend a networking dinner at a fancyish Indian restaurant. She'd been dreading it. This was exactly the kind of after-hours work event she hated, and she could think of a million ways she'd rather spend her Thursday evening. The guest list featured a conservative writer whose views Ann loathed, so she joked to a friend that she planned to show up late and say breezily, "Sorry, I had a 6pm abortion, and I thought I'd be done sooner!" But she had RSVP'd yes, and she knew Dayo would be there too. So Ann arrived on time.

When she walked into the restaurant, she was elated to find Aminatou already sitting at the table. Ann quickly claimed the seat next to her.

We fell into a rapid-fire conversation about everything *but* work. Denim skirts were our first and biggest point of disagree-ment. (Aminatou's position: they're never a good look. Ann's position: it depends. Aminatou has since softened on this issue.) Rather than going home after the meal ended, we headed to a nearby movie theater, where we watched a midnight screening of Beyoncé's star turn in the camp classic *Obsessed*. Aminatou had already seen it twice, but she wanted to spend more time with Ann, who had been meaning to see it but hadn't gotten around to it yet. We shared the conspiratorial thrill of being out late on a school night, having turned a networking event into a chance to enjoy some trashy pop culture together.

After that outing, our digital relationship began in earnest. We added each other on Gchat, the first big commitment in any new friendship at the time. Our first recorded email exchange is from less than a week after we met, when Aminatou—whom Ann had started calling Amina as other close friends did—forwarded an article about "Spring's Must-Have Denim Skirt." A few days later, Ann invited Aminatou to a cookout and trolled her by showing up in a denim skirt. But forget the skirt, Aminatou was more impressed that Ann had brought homemade deviled eggs.

Soon after our first unplanned friend dates, Aminatou sent Ann another fashion-blog post. (It's hard to overstate the role that fashion blogs played in our cultural consumption back in those pre-Instagram days.) "Ugh, denim skirt," she commented. Ann replied, "I like it! Can we still be friends?"

"Only if we hang out soon," Aminatou responded.

The denim skirt had become the first private meme in our friendship—a not-quite-joke we returned to again and again to signal to each other that we were paying attention. These relatively unimportant conversation topics were one way we began forging a shared sense of humor and taste.

The following month, Ann found out there was going to be a reality show about the lives of rich Manhattan teens, modeled on *Gossip Girl*. Of course she immediately sent the link to Aminatou, kicking off a volley of messages.

> **ANN:** Can we please have a date-night and watch this shit? to get us through the gossip girl off-season?
>
> **AMINATOU:** omg yes!! also can we hang out this weekend?

The Gmail trail doesn't lie: we were keeping up digitally, but always quickly proposing opportunities to spend time together in person. We both instinctively knew that we were still in that fragile, early phase of friendship when "out of sight" quickly becomes "out of mind." We had not gotten close yet, so if we stopped hanging out regularly, we would fade away from each other's lives. It's possible to go months without seeing a longtime friend and still feel close to them, but new friends require steady investment.

In our case, it helped that we are both what we like to call "social initiators": the ones who host the chaotic clothing swaps ("Friends of all body types welcome!"), the ones who will immediately send a calendar invite after someone says, "I've always wanted to go to that museum too." Our shared love language is making and keeping plans. We have both had our moments of feeling sad while sitting alone at home, but we also know how to channel that energy into reaching out to a friend. We are nothing if not proactive women.

As a consequence, we both get frustrated at social moochers. These are the people who are always complaining that no one wants to hang out with them yet never buy an extra movie ticket and invite someone to join, or send an email to suggest dates for a long-promised hang. Moochers passively rely on other people to fill their social calendar for them. But for us, it was easy to feel like our advances were quickly reciprocated in the early days of our friendship. Neither sat back and waited for the other to reach out first.

Being an initiator is not for extroverts only. Aminatou, an introvert, is not always energized by being around people. She learned early on that in order to have a social life she would need a plan. Setting up regularly scheduled one-on-one activities is one of the ways she gets to see her friends while also having a great deal of control over the social settings she finds herself in.

Structure helps many people with this phase of making friends: signing up for a class together, joining a league, or always seeing a movie on Friday night. (Some researchers will tell you that men are socialized to be more interested in forming friendships around doing activities together, while for many women activities are less important. Nonsense! We know women who love activities and men who love deep conversation too.) Whatever you pick can become your thing until the friendship is strong enough to survive without the external motivation to see each other. You'll know that's happened when you find it easy to propose other contexts to hang out in, and when your friendship expands to other settings.

If we hadn't followed up in a deliberate way, we would have

ended up as people who only pop up in each other's social-media feed because of a life event, prompting questions like, "Wait, who is this person flashing their engagement ring? Did we meet at a potluck once?" Almost immediately, though, we were making plans—and, even more important, we were actually following through. We resisted the cheap thrill of canceling last minute because we'd rather spend the night alone in our underwear eating snacks.

Eventually, we got close enough to spend time in our underwear *together* eating snacks.

G otta put in the face time" would become a refrain of Aminatou's in a later phase of our friendship, when we lived far apart from each other. But that maxim applies to the early days too. All significant friendships are founded on some serious time together.

You have probably heard about the 10,000-hour rule. According to the journalist Malcolm Gladwell, it's the number of hours required to master a skill. The number is based on research done by K. Anders Ericsson, a psychology professor at Florida State University who has said—twist!—that Gladwell misinterpreted his work. But the 10,000-hour idea became popular anyway, because we all want to know how to distill ambitious, difficult things down to their component inputs. "In cognitively demanding fields," Gladwell wrote, "there are no naturals."

In friendship, *our* cognitively demanding field, there are magic numbers too: 30 hours, 50 hours, 140 hours, and 300 hours. Jeffrey A. Hall, a researcher at the University of Kansas who has avoided being summarized by Gladwell, actually timed the early stages of friendships. Hall found that after 30 hours spent together, people said they considered each other "casual friends." After 50 hours, they would start referring to the other person as a "friend" with no qualifiers.

But it wasn't until 140 hours that people considered it a "good friendship." And "best friend" was a label people started using only after 300 hours together. That might seem like a lot of time, but it's actually only 12.5 days, just a little longer than a typical honeymoon trip. That's also basically enough time to watch a full season of a TV show together. In our case, it was approximately a dozen movies of questionable quality—some of which we endured only because of Aminatou's habit of bringing a Nalgene full of wine into the theater with her. It was many episodes of *NYC Prep* and *Entourage* and *RuPaul's Drag Race*. It was more than a few house parties and bar nights.

Our overlapping social circles made it easy to spend so much time together. The low-grade anxiety of "Have I forgotten to invite someone?" was a dominant feeling of our years in DC. Like a lot of postcollege 20-somethings in cities where there are job opportunities aplenty, we had a sprawling, interconnected social world. The group dynamic could be a blast. After Ann organized a holiday dinner for "some quality lady-time" at an over-the-top mansion that doubled as a restaurant, we spent hours taking photos of each other in dramatic poses around the venue. Later we found ourselves in a nearby Japanese spot doing karaoke to T.I. and Rihanna's "Live Your Life." We rolled deep to parties too, and no matter where we went, a good time was guaranteed because there were a lot of us. When you're still finding your place in the world or blowing off steam about the fact that you haven't figured it out yet, there's social safety in numbers.

Mostly, though, we could be found sitting in one of our apartments, doing next to nothing for hours. And it was definitely more than 300.

In the first year of our friendship, couch time was essential. After a quick exchange of "hey, what are you up to?" texts, Aminatou showed up at Ann's door. As soon as she stepped inside, she pulled off her bra through the sleeve of her shirt—obviously Ann was already free-boobing and in a pair of sweats. A DVD of questionable quality was queued up. Ann emerged from her tiny kitchen with snacks. She was into making pizza from scratch and adapting the many cheese-based appetizers of her Midwest upbringing to suit her adult vegetarian tastes. (Take it from Aminatou: if you don't have a Midwest diva in your life, you are really missing out on creamy, tangy, and super-spreadable dips.) We opened a bottle of wine or poured two glasses of whiskey, then sank into the luxurious feeling of the no-judgment zone. On other nights, it was Ann who turned up on Aminatou's doorstep, kicking off her shoes and curling up on one end of the couch. Aminatou had her own cheesy-dip repertoire. She had honed her queso-making skills in the heart of Texas and knew every store in town where you could get Ro-Tel, the key ingredient. Her margaritas were legendary, and even when there were snow drifts outside, they made Ann feel like she was on vacation in a warmer place.

There was something so satisfying about caring for each other in these little ways. For two women who had been raised by mothers who did all the cooking and took charge of entertaining, it felt transgressive to prepare dishes and select movies with only each other in mind—no husband or children in the equation. This simple ritual, usually just the two of us or a few other close friends, became a foundation of our friendship. Our private homes provided space away from the men who dominated our professional worlds. In our offices and at networking happy hours, they were dictating what was important, what was smart, what was funny, what was useful. There was something freeing about spending time alone with other women and allowing our own standards and definitions to flourish. Why would we go out at all when the people we were most excited to talk to were willing to walk to our house in a pair of leggings and stop by a corner store for a bottle of $6.99 Syrah and a bag of Tostitos along the way?

On a deeper level, all of this quality time at home also signaled that we were enough for each other. Reading the Sunday paper side by side was one of our favorite ways to spend time together. We didn't require small talk with a rotating cast of acquaintances to keep the conversation moving. We didn't need the potential thrill of getting hit on at a bar to be excited enough to show up. There was an immeasurable amount of comfort in doing nothing as an activity in its own right.

When we weren't together, we were constantly messaging each other during our work days. We would complain about office politics in real time, send each other links to things we were reading, and make plans for the moments after we shut down our computers, when we'd meet up in person to keep the conversation going.

Not every Big Friendship has a phase of intense bonding that looks exactly like ours, with its constant online and in-person contact. We've both had close friendships that tallied up their intimacy hours slowly, over several years, without a period of concentrated time together, or that found their deepness in digital contact. And the truth is that not every person we have spent hundreds of hours with was destined to be a friend for life. No two friendships are exactly alike.

But as we examine our friendship, and our reasons for wanting to make it last, this is a time period we return to again and again. When things got difficult between us later on, we would think back to the way we were able to build trust and intimacy during all those hours on the couch together. There was something about the way we told our life stories to each other. The details we selected. The hopes that we were only able to hint at but not yet see the contours of, and the dreams that we helped each other turn into goals and, later, realities. We didn't know it at the time, but forming this friendship was a way of setting a direction for our lives.

It's funny that high school, college, and the first years of adulthood are all identified as being formational years. Because for us, our late 20s and early 30s also represented a pretty radical amount of growth into our adult selves. We had achieved escape velocity from our upbringings and established a toehold in our careers, and we were starting to figure out adulthood. *How do you want to live? Who do you want to be?* These were questions we were answering together.

On our respective couches, we told each other the story of where we had come from, who we had met and loved along the way, and the fears and regrets we carried with us. And in the telling, we started to figure out where we wanted to go.

A minatou told Ann that she was born the oldest of three in a family from Guinea. She spent her childhood in Nigeria, and to live in Lagos in the 1990s was to have a very strong stomach for political chaos and all sorts of dysfunction. At an early age, Aminatou taught herself to read by deciphering every scrap of paper her parents left around the house: international newspapers, her father's boring reports from work, her mother's fashion magazines and crosswords. Getting lost in books and newspapers was a coping mechanism for her, a way to forget there wasn't any running water or electricity for weeks on end. Everyone eventually adapts, and Aminatou's parents were no exception. They created a sense of normalcy that Aminatou would come to appreciate even more deeply in later years.

Aminatou and her mother were very close—they had the same ease with people and the same boisterous laugh—but the only way she found she could relate to her father was by stepping into his very serious world. Some dads teach their kids how to throw a ball; Aminatou's dad taught her how to fold a broadsheet newspaper. Knowing something about everything was her way of finding things to discuss with him. Every night at the dinner table, her father would quiz her and her siblings about current events, sports, and the finer points of the European Union–West Africa Economic Partnership Agreement ("Europe's trap for Africa!"). It made sense that her parents were obsessed with information. They were expatriates who consumed every little bit of news from home and constantly wanted more, a habit that was passed on to Aminatou and her siblings.

Aminatou spent kindergarten through ninth grade in French international schools that emphasized to an almost comical level the importance of teamwork, mutual respect, and imagination. Even though her preferred recess activity was chatting up the school librarian and requesting new books, she could get along with pretty much anyone. Even her elementary-school bully became a middle-school bestie, and they still keep in touch.

Aminatou grew up watching her parents convening all sorts of gatherings, which is how she learned to overcome her shyness and become a social initiator. Managing cross-continental friendships, in wartime or peacetime, was just a way of life. On weekends, the whole family would venture to her dad's office or a telecom center to make calls to seemingly everyone in the Guinean diaspora. In 1996, her family got a landline, a milestone so important that Aminatou can still describe every button on that telephone. Aminatou's parents would stay up for hours—truly, hours—dialing foreign numbers until they connected with someone. Both of her parents were avid letter writers to family and friends back home, and her mother would often dictate the text to Aminatou. There was no reliable mail service in her part of West Africa, so letters would be sent with friends who were passing through. Aminatou's parents never made the time or effort seem like a chore, and they showed Aminatou that it was possible to have significant long-distance relationships. She saw firsthand that keeping in touch was an art. And her parents were masters of it.

In middle school, when Aminatou's friend Antoine moved to Madagascar, the two of them figured out how to use the diplomatic mail service to their advantage. When that wasn't possible, they would entrust every adult they knew going anywhere between Antananarivo and Lagos with their correspondence. It was haphazard. Letters got lost. Packages showed up years later. In time, phone calls got easier to make. They could go months with no communication and then catch up where they had left off. Antoine was Aminatou's first significant long-distance friend, and would definitely not be her last. Even though Aminatou is embarrassed by her terrible handwriting—her penmanship took a nosedive after French school—she makes it a point to always send postcards on her travels (no better way to learn a city than having to find the post office), because she knows firsthand the thrill of opening the mailbox and finding a missive from a friend instead of just bills and junk mail.

In an early display of ambition, Aminatou convinced her parents to let her go to boarding school. The compromise they set was that it would have to be close enough that they could pop in easily. They settled on a Christian academy with an American school curriculum in central Nigeria. Aminatou took an English immersion program in the summer and aced the entrance exam. Most of her classmates were children of missionaries, so the school was very different from the secular French education she was used to and the Islam practiced by her family. Her parents downplayed the inevitable culture shock she would feel. "Christians run great schools!" they always said. "Respect their beliefs, nod along when they pray, and everything will be fine." Incredibly polite optimism has always been the Sow family stance.

At the American-run boarding school, she had to make a few adjustments, like giving up her beloved fountain pens for

pencils and BIC 4-Color ballpoint pens. She almost didn't recognize herself without blue ink stains all over her fingers. She
traded in her leather *cartable* for a more age-appropriate leather
satchel, but she refused to give in to backpack culture. She was an
early adopter of athleisure and wore her slides everywhere, along
with her beloved chunky knit cardigans and bold-print Naf Naf
sweaters when it was cold. Not everything about the new school
was different, though. Aminatou was still surrounded by Third-
Culture Kids just like her. In this group, there was nothing exceptional about growing up in a culture other than the one their
parents were raised in, or living outside of the country named
on their passport. The idea of growing up on one street for your
whole life or having attended a single school was completely foreign to kids like her.

She was an Amnesty International letter writer, volunteered
at the fistula clinic in town, and taught the women at the local
prison how to read and write, even though the authorities sanc-
tioned only Bible study and crochet lessons. Aminatou helped the
women smuggle letters out to their families and lawyers. When
her boarding school revived its draconian dress code, Aminatou
didn't understand why everyone thought this was acceptable. She
demanded to know why it applied only to girls' clothing, and she
was outraged when male teachers would ask girls to bend over or
kneel to prove that their clothes met their sexist standards. Aminatou still can't crochet, but Amnesty letters, the fistula clinic, and
going up against school administrators formed the foundation of
her feminist beliefs. Nobody came to the Iraq War protest she
organized, but it didn't faze her. She was amused when a classmate she hadn't seen in more than a decade recently asked her

how she'd managed to be so secure in her political beliefs at such a young age. She didn't miss a beat: "My world was bigger than high school."

College loomed large as a utopia where she would be surrounded by kindred spirits and could make the kind of adult friendships she'd always idealized, and Aminatou was counting down the days. Going to a prestigious European university was the expectation for accomplished kids in her family, but she wanted to plant a flag somewhere farther away from what she knew. She wanted to go to America.

An acceptance letter arrived from every college she applied to, including the Ivies that her guidance counselor and parents urged her to consider. Aminatou settled on the University of Texas at Austin because the brochure said it had 50,000 undergraduates. Her high school graduating class had 29 people in it, and everyone knew everyone's families. She wanted to be anonymous, a number on a student ID.

Aminatou arrived at the University of Texas alone, and she was amused that everyone else who was new on campus had their entire family in tow for move-in day. She and her parents had said an emotional goodbye at the airport when she boarded the flight to Austin, but it had never occurred to her that they would actually come on the trip. Her parents had taken her this far, and it was now her turn to start a new life, in a new country. It was her first inkling that her life was very different from the average Texas college student's, and the first experience of many in America where she was made to feel that there might be something unusual about her background.

She started college in the spring semester, and it seemed

everyone had already picked their roommate for the next year and had a very solid group of friends. But she was determined to find her people. A few weeks later, Aminatou walked past a recruitment table for a campus organization and found herself intrigued by its motto: "Spirit, Love, Service, and Friendship." Sure, why not? She did her research, and Texas Spirits was basically a sorority for nerdy girls who aspired to shatter glass ceilings wherever they went. They raised money for charity, wore burnt-orange scarves to UT football and basketball games, and giggled their way through frat parties and sleepovers. The selection process was intimidating, but of course she got in. To this day, Aminatou loves an exclusive group and has always felt she could easily infiltrate any members' club to meet interesting people. It's the self-assurance that comes with being a worldly person.

The Spirits soon dominated her social calendar. Austin was the perfect backdrop for the sweet swim dates, dance parties, and margarita-fueled nights Aminatou couldn't even have imagined would make her so happy. It was the Spirits who first taught her the magic of hanging out with a big group of women, something she had never really experienced. Even though membership rules dictated they tap out of the organization in their sophomore year, their bond was cemented and would carry them through graduation and beyond. These were the friends Aminatou had pictured when she was in high school daydreaming about college life. They were with her as she took her first stumbles into adulthood.

When another freshman invited her to a "spiritual retreat" put on by her church, Aminatou didn't quite know what to expect but went anyway. When she walked into the den of the south Austin house, she saw a bodacious blonde belting out the lyrics to "Mr. Jones" and playing along on the piano: "Starin' at this yellow-haired girl." Aminatou immediately wanted to know her.

Aminatou learned her name was Brittany, and even though they had met at a church-sanctioned event, on their first friend date they talked approximately 0 percent about Jesus and 100 percent about music and TV. When Aminatou didn't return to the church, she had no doubt that their friendship would survive. And it did. It was Brittany who almost always picked her up from the airport when she returned to school. Two years later, when Aminatou's mother died, it was Brittany who would sing Frou Frou's "Let Go" to soothe her when she was crying. No matter how many times Aminatou played Coldplay's "Don't Panic" and Iron & Wine's version of "Such Great Heights" in the car, Brittany never got annoyed. Good friends let grieving friends play sad-sack indie jams from the *Garden State* soundtrack with no judgment. Brittany had crossed over into Big Friendship territory.

Those college friendships had made Aminatou into the person Ann eventually met. Sitting on the opposite end of the sofa, Ann loved hearing Aminatou tell the story of her life in nonchronological details and hilarious anecdotes. Every time Aminatou revealed a surprising part of her past, Ann was thrilled. "You volunteered at a fistula clinic?" "You speak five languages?" "You had a *Christian phase*!?"

Ann began developing a narrative about Aminatou: her new friend was a woman of global experience, able to thrive in any situation and impress any crowd, emotionally resilient, and possessed of a firm, unwavering opinion about almost everything. Ann could see in Aminatou many traits she admired in herself, and many more qualities she had always aspired to but never quite achieved.

On a deeper level she was thrilled by what Aminatou's entrance into her life represented. In a way no friend ever had before, Aminatou felt like Ann's gateway to a wider world.

O ne reason Ann hung on every word of Aminatou's story was that she was fascinated by how much it diverged from her own. While also the oldest of three children, Ann was born in Iowa to parents who had never lived more than a few hours' drive from where they were raised. Her Catholic family tried to instill in her many religious values that never really took (sorry, it's just a wafer!). She stopped going to confession at an early age because she sensed that the sin of sassing her parents could not be absolved by a priest's blessing and a few Hail Marys. But other values from her upbringing remain deeply ingrained, like respecting a serious work ethic and really sticking with your people long-term. Her parents each had a few college friends they kept in touch with, and her mother was also an avid letter writer. Ann's family was often at Resurrection Church, or sharing casseroles with families whose kids were her classmates at Resurrection School. It was all very insular, and to this day, Ann feels confined by formal groups.

When her family moved to a new ranch-style brick house when Ann was 12, it was just a few blocks away from their old ranch-style brick house. Her primary experiences of the world beyond her small town came from the TV shows she watched and the many books she read, which were set in exotic locales like the New York City suburbs and Canadian boarding schools. She would often borrow her mother's adult library card, which let her check out 20 books at a time. (The children's card maxed out at 10.) Once a year, her grandma would bring her along on a day trip to Chicago to see a play or a musical. The trips were arranged through a local bank as an activity for retirees, so Ann would be the lone kid on a bus full of gray-haired ladies. She loved it. This was her ticket to the big city—which she'd read about in books like *Harriet the Spy*—and it offered her the first glimpses of the kind of life she wanted to live as an adult, which was very different from the one her parents had chosen.

If you want to know what Ann looked like as a teenager, picture the classic '90s cartoon *Daria*, but way more physically awkward at a gangly six feet two inches tall. Her parents did not approve of her self-selected thrift-store wardrobe, so she would smuggle her destroyed vintage corduroys, which met the dress-code requirements on a technicality, and then change in the bathroom at school. Her best friend Bridget, whom she had met in junior-high math class, lived next door to their high school but would drive all the way to Ann's house to pick her up in the morning, usually blasting Prince from her two-tone beige Nissan. Like Ann, Bridget had no interest in school sports or religion, and they started an extremely premature countdown to graduation. They spent hours in Bridget's basement, sipping LaCroix while watching old Hitchcock movies and reruns of *Absolutely Fabulous*. If she wasn't at Bridget's, Ann was with her other bestie Josh. They worked on the school newspaper together and could reliably be found special-ordering CDs at the local music store, or at a strip-mall coffee shop reading the *New York Times*, sipping sugary lattes and making plans for when they'd leave their suffocating town and life would truly begin. Both of these friendships are still going strong, perhaps because they always felt rooted in the future as much as in the present.

Maybe it was all that reading. Or maybe it was because social-justice Catholics were the only role models from Ann's religious education that she actually respected. (Shout out to Óscar Romero and Dorothy Day.) But however it happened, Ann developed a social conscience pretty early. As a teen, she ran her school chapter of Amnesty International, meaning she'd get to school early to write letters on behalf of political prisoners in Russia and Chad. She planned an annual benefit concert called, regrettably, Jamnesty, and she was once the sole person at the death-penalty protest that she herself had organized. She desperately wanted to be someone who was involved in the world beyond their hometown.

The day Ann's parents dropped her off at college remains among the happiest of her life. She was finally free to begin writing her own story, far from the confines of her upbringing. She had always wanted to be a writer, so she had picked the University of Missouri for its undergraduate journalism program. She was definitely not the only person at the death-penalty protest anymore. And, like her, everyone was eager to write for the campus newspapers (yes, there were multiple) and primed to eventually compete for an impossibly tiny number of entry-level reporting jobs. Suddenly, Ann was the norm.

She befriended a couple of photojournalism students, Lara and Gracy, who lived in her cinder-block dorm and shared her taste in music and movies. Once a week, they indulged in an off-campus dinner at the local vegetarian restaurant Main Squeeze. The following year, these women became Ann's first chosen roommates, and together they experienced the joys and frustrations of cohabitation. They threw a raucous cocktail party where someone did an accidental backflip over the banister (she lived to tell the tale) and let touring indie-rock bands crash on their floor and lumpy couch—which was later incinerated after Gracy's boyfriend fell asleep on it with a lit cigarette. Their bonds were forged by countless late-night conversations in the house's weird upstairs kitchen, over reheated burritos and ramen noodles. Ann reveled in the feeling that they had selected each other out of thousands of people on campus.

In her senior year, Ann was recruited to join a fundraiser to send several busloads of Missouri feminists to a protest march against the Bush administration in DC. It was these women who showed Ann by example what it looks like to call yourself a feminist. Thanks to them, she finally read the iconic writer bell hooks! These friendships felt deep from the start because they were underpinned by shared values. And even if Ann was extremely stressed out about how she would make a career as an "objective" journalist who was also an impassioned feminist, she was also grateful to these new friends for introducing the complication.

Stories like these didn't just fill Aminatou in on where Ann was coming from. As Aminatou listened, she sensed the expansive possibilities of this budding friendship. She was intrigued that she could share so much emotional and cultural DNA with someone she had just met. Aminatou loved that Ann was never judgmental and incredibly independent-minded. She was not shy about expressing her needs and wants, and she set clear expectations about her place in the world. This made Aminatou feel that she could prioritize herself as well.

We hung on to each other's every word. But we didn't realize that we were doing more than telling the stories of ourselves. We were starting to tell a joint story about who we were together.

F or all the obvious differences between us, it was hard not to notice how similar we were.

We grew up thousands of miles apart, but we were both from relatively conservative cultures where the first questions of young women were often "What's your dad's name? What does he do?" We had both always wanted life to take us far from home. We were usually reading between one and three different books at any given time. We were accustomed to people making rude comments about our height and weight, respectively. And even though we complained about how hard it was to find cute clothes that fit, or confessed how awkward we sometimes felt in our own skin, it was always clear that we didn't hate our bodies. We weren't trying to change them. We shared a desire to be women who take up a lot of space and refuse to apologize for it. We loved eating in restaurants alone, preferably at the bar. Our hearts soared every time we discovered something we had in common. *Where has she been my whole life?* we thought. *How am I so lucky to have found this person?*

We were creating our "story of sameness," as the linguist Deborah Tannen calls it. In her book *You're the Only One I Can Tell*, she notes that people who were socialized as women tend to pepper their conversations with phrases like "The same thing happened to me" and "I know, I feel the same way." Sometimes, Tannen observes, this process can be subtly competitive—a way of one-upping each other or minimizing the other person's experience by quickly saying you've done that too. But it doesn't have to be, and we can honestly say we never felt anything but admiration and curiosity in those early days.

We felt so lucky to have found someone on our exact wavelength. What we didn't realize was that we were actually *creating* the wavelength. Our ideas about showing emotion, relating to other friends, expressing vulnerabilities, and handling conflict were forming in relation to each other. We were both adept at hiding our insecurities and quick to dismiss or downplay them with a joke or snarky comment. Acquaintances and casual friends tended to view us both as "strong" people who had our shit together. It was possible for us to crack our hard shells open and expose some soft underbelly to each other because we could share a knowing laugh about how weird it was for both of us. And we were self-described "low-drama mamas"—a term our friend group used for women who avoided gossiping about and picking fights with other women. It was a way of distancing ourselves from the stereotype that women are all dramatic and eager to make a big deal out of nothing. Our joint story was that together we were fierce about our ideals but also easygoing. We strived to be your favorite lady's favorite ladies. We weren't just spending a lot of time together and recognizing our points of sameness. We were amplifying and doubling down on them.

But with the self-knowledge that only hindsight and therapy can bring, we have come to recognize that we are actually very different people—especially on an emotional level. We didn't notice right away because we were so focused on our story of sameness. And later, when other parts of our relationship got difficult, those deep differences blindsided us.

We didn't realize that we were able to open up to each other in those early days *despite* our differences. Aminatou shares intimate details of her life only with people she believes will be close to her in the future. Ann tends to think that everyone else's problems are bigger than hers and that can make her reluctant to go into detail about her own. But we got close anyway. We didn't consider it a risk at the time, nor did it feel like we were overcoming something difficult when we shared with each other.

This feeling of safety was at the very heart of what made our friendship work.

THREE

..

Chosen Family

I t took only a few months for us to grow extremely attached to each other. We have no idea if that was moving fast or an average timeline, because friendship is so rarely studied as an intimate bond. The research on close relationships is mostly based on parents and children or romantic couples.

In her dissertation on best friendships, communications professor Emily Langan studied whether attachment theory—a way of describing how children bond with their parents—might also apply to platonic intimate relationships. She received "massive pushback" from her colleagues, who argued that this kind of attachment exists only in families. Langan, however, says that close friendships have some characteristics that aren't so different from stable families. First, friends who are attached have a desire to see a lot of each other and know what's going on in each other's lives. Second, the friends provide a secure base for each other—meaning the friendship allows them to go out and explore other friendships, romantic relationships, new jobs, anything that might feel scary but ultimately positive, because they can look over their shoulder and know their friend is there for them. And third, they offer each other a safe harbor. When things go wrong for one friend, the other loyally and dependably steps up to offer support.

We didn't know a thing about attachment theory back when we met, but Langan's dissertation could have been written about us. We were obviously seeing a lot of each other and were up-to-date on each other's lives. But it's the "secure base" aspect of Langan's theory that rings especially true.

Even though we hadn't signed a piece of paper committing to love and support each other, we felt a sureness about our bond and its future. We slid easily into the gaps in each other's lives that were left by exes, absentee long-distance friends, and disconnected biological family members. We were determined to do better by each other.

At the time we met, Ann was living with the boyfriend she had met back in San Francisco and moved to DC for. She was not the type to air every little annoyance about her romantic relationship, but she had told Aminatou about the travails of cohabitation: her boyfriend's tendency to polish off the contents of the fridge without shopping for replacements, the mismatch of his night-owl tendencies to her solid-eight-hours sleep schedule, their standoff about who was going to mop the grimy bathroom floor and scrub the soap scum off the tub. Somehow, when she talked to Aminatou about this, it seemed less like routine complaining and more like an important discussion about living her feminist values. The friendship was secure enough that she could share her grievances without worrying that Aminatou would get weird around her boyfriend or judge her for staying with him.

But it was more than that. Aminatou had created a new secure base in Ann's life. All those hours Ann had spent sharing her hopes and fears with Aminatou had given her a new perspective on what emotional intimacy really felt like—and Ann recognized it was missing with her boyfriend. Her friendships gave her a feeling of security that allowed her to contemplate leaving this long-term romantic relationship.

And so, when Ann finally decided it was time to end things, a few of her older, long-distance friends were shocked. But Aminatou, who knew every dirty detail of the bathroom standoff, wasn't surprised at all. She also understood the deeper reasons Ann was unhappy. The truth was Ann had spent most of her 20s in romantic relationships that had shaped her in ways she wasn't always thrilled about. She longed to live alone. More than anything, she wanted to see who she was, and how she'd change, if she was single and not defined in relation to a boyfriend.

Aminatou was already a secure base, but she soon became a safe harbor. When Ann finally asked her boyfriend to move out—which kicked off a messy, drawn-out process involving several tearful relationship discussions in public places—Aminatou was her rock. She spent hours listening to Ann recount every emotional twist and turn and helped Ann through her guilt about being the instigator of the split. Aminatou wasn't just a friend who was lending a sympathetic ear. Ann was certain that Aminatou was right there with her in every moment, empathizing with her heartache. She could leave her boyfriend without worrying that she'd be lonely or unsupported.

But Aminatou also never told a lie. When Ann pulled the classic white-girl move of cutting her bangs too short in the wake of the breakup, Aminatou did not sugarcoat things. Within moments of witnessing Ann's unfortunate new rockabilly look, she simply said, "Well, I guess we're not wearing polka dots until this grows out." It was a deft way of affirming that she was in Ann's corner (the "we") and also not lying to her about the impulsive haircut. A few weeks later, when Ann made plans to do the unthinkable and get a drink with her ex to discuss the state of the breakup, Aminatou was there for her again.

AMINATOU: MIDDLE EAST PEACE PROCESS
ANN: srsly. also, i feel weird about what to wear tonight. obvs
  i wanna look fab. but is that, like, not ok? am i supposed to
  just look "average" for drinks w/ the ex? so many fashion
  questions.
AMINATOU: hahaha no. you gotta look like a million dollars.

Aminatou was not only on call for support that night ("i can call/text something bogus that can be your out"), but she also holed up with a few other close friends in a nearby bar so Ann could meet up with them immediately afterward. Drinks with the ex did not go well, and when Ann showed up in tears, the group was waiting. The next day, she emailed them in gratitude: "after i parted ways with him and i met up with you lovelies, the contrast was SO stark. i really think that's why i was crying so hard. . . . i know i said it in just a few words yesterday, but i wanted to say it in more words today: thankyouthankyouthankyou for being such forces of hope and light and love and joy in my life."

Aminatou even managed to turn a sad post-breakup IKEA trip into a happy memory, putting her safety at risk while Ann worked out her feelings behind the wheel of a U-Haul. "My blind spot, your problem," Ann said as she tore across the freeways of Northern Virginia at a speed that can only be described as "newly single." Aminatou survived one of Ann's characteristic low-blood-sugar meltdowns by pushing her to eat some Swedish Fish at just the right moment in the checkout lane. And together we carried a huge chest of drawers—which Aminatou had managed to snag for Ann from a mutual friend who was getting rid of it—up three flights of stairs through sheer determination. Pretty good for two women who are not into CrossFit. Years later, it would take three of our male friends, struggling mightily, to bring that chest of drawers down the stairs again. It was clear: we were superwomen and could do anything together.

In less than a year of friendship, Aminatou had opened up to Ann about romantic dramas, money, and health. This was faster than usual for her. But she still found it difficult to talk about her relationship with her father. Aminatou hadn't seen him in quite some time and he was coming for a visit from Belgium, where her family had lived for the past decade. In her family, as in a lot of immigrant families, parents and children often talk to each other in terms of accomplishments. Aminatou wasn't in graduate school and she had no career to speak of. She didn't feel like she had anything going on or anything to show for her life. In the years since her mom died, it felt like her personal relationship with her father had withered. The prospect of this lunch was stressful on so many levels.

She made a reservation at a fancy restaurant, and she remembers saying a small prayer before walking in: "God, let this not be a disaster." Wishful thinking. They sat outside on the patio, across from each other at the table. The conversation was lively whenever they talked about the news and world events. But things felt strained whenever they turned to her work or their other family members. Aminatou missed her mother's soft touch in moments like these, and it was obvious that her father did too. Her mother would have been a great buffer, helping bridge the emotional divide between father and daughter. They were both still grieving her, and without her, they didn't have a way of talking about their sadness.

Aminatou's father hadn't said anything unkind or that she was a failure, but the lunch still felt like a complete disaster. It did not help that Aminatou was walking around with an undiagnosed anxiety disorder. In a fugue state afterward, she ended up on Ann's couch.

When Ann asked how it went, Aminatou could barely produce coherent words and started hyperventilating. She cried. Hard. At the time, it felt like a completely shocking thing to do. She rarely cried, even in front of people she'd known for decades, and she'd known Ann for only a few months. Out of the corner of her eye, she searched Ann's face for signs of annoyance or judgment. Nothing. Well, not nothing, but Ann didn't seem the least bit fazed that a hysterical woman was wailing on her couch. (Honestly, it was probably a regular amount of dignified crying, but all feelings are dramatic to Aminatou.) Ann was calm and steady. She didn't need to know every single detail of why the lunch felt so disastrous—all she needed was to see that her friend was upset.

Ann stood up, walked into the bedroom, and called to Aminatou, "Do you want a Xanax?"

Yes. Aminatou very much needed a Xanax. But more than anything, she had needed to know that being overly emotional would not cause this new friend to run away. Growing up, she had internalized the idea that strong displays of emotion were to be avoided at all cost—otherwise people wouldn't want to be around you. In that moment, Ann had passed a test that Aminatou hadn't realized she was administering. It was also when Aminatou realized that she needed to open her eyes to the fact that Ann was showing up for her in a real way. She settled into a new level of security in the friendship.

I t's impossible to say exactly when the shift happened, but we had become more than besties. Our mutual friends started joining our names with an ampersand, a sure linguistic sign that you are publicly tied to another person. *Ann & Amina. Amina & Ann.* We became a vital part of each other's daily support system, and we were grounded in the intimately mundane.

> **AMINATOU:** have eaten 5 bags of fruit snacks today. this cant be good
> **ANN:** poop or consequences

We had keys to each other's apartments. We often made each other dinner after a long day at work. And any time difficulties with our families of origin cropped up, we would remind each other, "Ugh, this is why chosen fam is everything."

Chosen family is not a label we invented. For decades, the LGBTQ community has used the term to describe people who decide to play significant roles in each other's lives for the long haul. When most people think of a family, they often still think of getting married and having children—two life choices that have historically been denied to LGBTQ folks. The use of "chosen family" was first studied by the anthropologist Kath Weston, who was researching kinship in the gay and lesbian communities in San Francisco in the 1980s. She published her research in a 1991 book, *Families We Choose*, which describes the way these chosen families shared resources, co-parented children, and supported each other through illness, notably during the AIDS crisis. At the time, some critics pointed out that because many of the people who pioneered the use of the term "chosen family" were rejected by their families of origin, they did not have much choice in the matter at all. The psychology professor Karen Blair notes that, for queer people in the late 20th century, the choice to create alternative bonds outside of one's biological family was often "borne out of necessity." But for us—and for many other people who use that term to describe their kinship bonds today—"chosen family" describes intimate relationships that are freely selected.

We listed each other as the emergency contact on our HR forms at work. We hosted parties together. We planned Friendsgiving menus. We were in our mid- and late 20s, peak wedding years among our large and far-flung friend groups. Without romantic partners to split expenses with, we were feeling the financial strain. And so, as our friend circles overlapped more and more, we increasingly attended weddings together. We shared hotel rooms. We coordinated our looks for the ceremony. (Animal prints for Kate and Brant's. Pink florals for Phoebe and Eric's. Chic black for Gabe and Michael's.) We gave wedding gifts jointly, signed, "Love, the Sow-Friedmans." Of course, you can be super close to a friend even if you aren't attending weddings as a pair or listing each other as an emergency contact. No two Big Friendships are alike. But this was our way of being a chosen family. We didn't need a lavish ceremony to tell the world that we were a duo.

Our choice to show up at weddings as a family unit wasn't just a cute stunt. It was an extension of our political beliefs that friendship is a relationship that's equal in importance to romantic and family bonds.

The historian Stephanie Coontz, who studies marriage and family structures in America and Western Europe, notes that, in the same way that societies have changed their definitions and expectations of family and romantic relationships over time, the expectations for friendship have evolved over centuries. (Until we called her, Coontz, who makes her living studying intimate relationships, had never been asked about how marriage and family structures affect friendships!) She gave us a brief history of how powerful people in Western society have set the standards for friendship, and how people of other class and racial groups often developed their own variations on those standards.

In the 16th and 17th centuries, marriages tended to be arranged to make political or economic alliances or to create community solidarities. "Love was nice if it came afterwards, but it was not considered a good reason for marriage," Coontz says. "And so friendships were very different and perhaps more emotionally central to people."

In the late 18th and 19th centuries, when it became common to marry for love, middle-class people began worrying that the couple would have no reason to stay married if their affections dissipated. With more men working outside the home, women were newly responsible for domestic life, and the idea of separate spheres developed. This was an early version of the notion that men are from Mars and women are from Venus, with different sets of inherent skills and social roles. All men were now supposed to be ambitious, hard-nosed, and interested in public matters. And women were supposed to be sexually pure, emotional, and nurturing. If men and women are two sides of a coin, the theory went, they must get married and stay married in order to access the supposedly innate traits of the other. *You complete me.* "So this led to this intense romanticization of the other," Coontz says, "but also it opened the way for a real flowering of male/male and female/female friendships, because those were the people that you had everything in common with, supposedly."

In letters to each other during the 19th century, some women refer to men as "the grosser sex." Friendship, not romantic relationships, were a place where women felt free to be themselves and express their emotions. And intense female friendships, even those that might seem erotic to modern eyes, were accepted because women were supposedly so pure that they wouldn't have sex with each other, even if they slept in the same bed all night. If a woman professed to have a crush on another woman, it wasn't seen as commentary on her sexuality. "Men also had very intense friendships," Coontz says. She points to letters in which men who identified as heterosexual "talk about falling to sleep with their head lying peacefully on the breast of their good friend." But this idea of men and women as opposites had a chilling effect on friendships between men and women.

Toward the end of the 19th century, middle-class Americans began to recognize that these ideas made it hard for men and women to construct intimate marriages. Gradually, middle-class Americans adopted the practice of dating, which had already emerged in the working class. It became more acceptable for women to appear in public, even to work. This led to the rise of what was called "companionate marriage." It was not yet the era of "I married my best friend," but it became accepted that women and men should share activities—though emphasis was still placed on women adapting to men's interests—and pursue a mutually fulfilling sex life. Ironically, this new emphasis on sexuality meant that same-sex behaviors that previously had been perceived as merely affectionate—like holding hands or falling asleep on the breast of your good friend—were now sexualized. This dealt a huge blow to close same-sex friendships, which suddenly became less acceptable as they came to be viewed as a threat to male-female romantic partnership.

"In the early twentieth century [there was] a huge campaign by the so-called experts to wipe out the idea of these girlish crushes that used to be considered perfectly acceptable and kind of fun," Coontz says. "And men found themselves under suspicion if they walked down the street the way they used to, with an arm around each other's shoulders." Women in close relationships with other women could be labeled lesbians — and some of them undoubtedly really were lesbians. This was before the gay rights movement made it safer to come out. It can be really hard to tell which historical bestie pairs were indeed platonic pals, which were, in fact, romantic partners, and which fell somewhere in between.

Some of the old ideas about gender difference persisted, giving a conflicting set of messages to women seeking friendship: get close to other women (you're built for friendship), but not too close (you don't want to be seen as lesbians), use those friendships to provide support until the day you find a man to marry, then abandon those relationships on your wedding day, when you will be expected to fully devote yourself to hearth and home. Coontz interviewed many women who came of age in the 1950s and '60s, who told her that their youthful friendships with other women revolved around trying to meet a husband. These women expressed sadness that, once everyone was married off, they had little to talk about with their old friends anymore.

"So this was the real low point in the history of female friendships," Coontz says, "and of course, by that time, male friendships were really off the table. Men were increasingly expected to get any emotional support they needed from their wife, not from other men." By the 1970s and '80s, as middle-class women returned to the workforce and sought political and economic equality, they began to reject the idea that they should abandon their friendships upon getting married. And people of all genders started figuring out how passionate romantic love could coexist with passionate friendship bonds.

It's pretty clear to us that, as a society, we are still working on this. We are trying to let go of a lot of outdated ideas about what it means to be a man or a woman, a friend or a spouse. On a personal level, the two of us have always wanted to be independent women who don't center our conversations on men. We want people of every gender to be free to feel the expansive joy of intimate friendships. We want to have a supportive network of friends, fulfilling romantic relationships, and strong family bonds—while still charting our own course in the world.

Q uickly and easily, we had simply become enmeshed in every part of each other's lives. We didn't feel like we had a single secret from each other. This feeling was recognizable only by absences: the absence of misunderstandings, the absence of shame or fear in sharing things, the absence of insecurity. It wasn't that we made a conscious pledge to be friends forever. It's that we accepted a truth deep within ourselves that our lives, from that point forward, would always include each other. Anything else was unimaginable.

Much like there is a superficial story of our origin, there is also a superficial story of chosen family. When we thought about our own chosen family and its future, we considered only the good parts. We never paused to think about what chosen family might mean if—or, more realistically, *when*—things got difficult. We have yet to hear about family, chosen or not, without a single fight or long-simmering resentment. Families are sources of love and support, but they also have moments marked by disappointment and awkwardness. Most families don't just have beautiful rituals; they also have destructive patterns.

It didn't even occur to us. During our first years together, we didn't have a single fight—not even once—over something trivial.

If pressed, we couldn't name a single fault about each other. We hadn't been tested yet. We were not assessing *why* our friendship worked so well. We were not thinking about the long-term implications of claiming each other as family. We were just enjoying it.

And for the moment, that was OK.

FOUR

..

I Don't Shine
If You Don't Shine

Aminatou remembers the day one of her managers told her that he wouldn't mentor her.

She was in his office at the think tank, a cramped space cluttered with boxes and dry cleaning hanging on the door. Aminatou had been looking forward to this meeting with him, because she thought he was finally going to take an interest in her work and encourage some goal setting. But instead he said, essentially, that she had gone to the wrong schools, that women didn't distinguish themselves in policy, and that his time was better spent working with the men in her cohort. He said all of this in such a casual, matter-of-fact way that it took Aminatou a long time to understand just how sexist he was being. Mostly she was worried.

When she was hired, they had told her they would sponsor her visa. She now found herself questioning their commitment. Why would they go through the effort for an employee who wasn't even worth mentoring?

She was also crushed about what this would mean for her career. But she would soon learn that she wasn't alone in lacking mentorship.

A few blocks away, Ann was regularly frustrated by her own bosses, who referred to even the most senior woman on staff as "sweetie" and sometimes treated the younger women in the office as personal secretaries. When Ann worked up the nerve to suggest to one of the magazine's founders that he wasn't paying enough attention to ideas put forth by women writers, he defensively told her, "My first wife was in the women's movement!" Ann nearly spat out her coffee.

Even though we worked in different industries, the early days of our professional lives felt remarkably similar. Our parents had taught us that you go to school, you work hard, and you rise through the ranks—but that wasn't proving true for us or our friends as we tried to start our careers in a recession economy. We were both ambitious but had few role models to guide us.

In a study that won't surprise anyone who's looked around an office in corporate America, 63 percent of women say they've never had a mentor. And it's not just a problem for women; it's a generational one. According to a Harvard Business School study, "Everyone we spoke with over age 40 could name a mentor in his or her professional life, but younger people often could not." We were getting tired of waiting for someone older and wiser to help us find our path forward, and so we started to look to our peers to exchange information about jobs, salaries, and obstacles. Over watered-down happy-hour cocktails and bar snacks that passed as dinner, we started to understand that everyone was just doing their best and faking it along the way.

We knew that, as women, the early years of our careers were particularly important. This was when we were supposed to be building earning power, because after age 35 or so—and certainly if you start having kids—the wage gap really starts yawning open. We felt a sense of urgency about building our salary base. Over and over again we assured each other that it was OK to want more, to ask for more, and to follow through even if we felt weird or unsure about it.

While we don't select friends because they might help us advance our careers, here's the dirty capitalist truth: friendship has been the source of some of our biggest professional leaps. We are women for whom work is a huge part of our identity, in a way that wasn't true for either of our mothers. Friends are how we've figured out the salary we deserve and how to negotiate for it. They've been a source of solace when our bosses shortchanged us, and they've been the inspiration to keep going when, having moved up, we *become* the bosses and feel like imposters.

Aminatou often jokes that we have steamrolled each other to success, but really, it's simple: We love and admire our friends so much, we want the world to respect and reward them for their efforts. We want our friends to demand more for themselves. And get it.

A couple of months after that awful meeting about mentorship, Aminatou was told that the think tank couldn't afford to keep her on staff anymore. This was alarming for many reasons, but especially because she no longer had a sponsor for her visa, which meant she was about to lose her legal status in the country. There was only one month left in her work authorization, and she had just signed a year lease. America was home now. If she were to be deported, it would be to Guinea, a country she had never lived in and knew she wouldn't be safe in. She was devastated.

Thankfully, over the past year in DC, she had built a solid network of new friends. She fired off an email to them, explaining her situation. "This could not come at a worse time," she wrote. "The best way for me to be able to stay in the country will be through employment. If you have any leads, please let me know. If you have referrals to an immigration service/attorney, I will gladly take those as well because I need to discuss my options in detail. Worst-case scenario: I leave sometime in November back to Belgium and eventually Guinea until I get into grad school which will probably be in Europe because apparently the American Dream costs way too much $$$."

Everyone stepped up to help. Of course they did. Within days Aminatou had a few promising job leads. As the immigration clock counted down, she was worried about where exactly she would go when America shut her out. Another friend connected her to a lawyer who told her she had a credible claim for asylum, and he agreed to take on her case pro bono. He explained it would be a very long process, but it was possible that she could be granted asylum and stay in the country.

If Los Angeles is a town where people's first question is "How are you?" and in New York it's "Who are you?" the first question in DC is definitely "What do you do?" Aminatou was unemployed, and she was often surrounded by people looking over her shoulder to see if there was someone more important in the room. Dealing with strangers' judgment of her new reality was hard, but she thought it would sting more than it actually did. Mostly, it reinforced her sense that she needed to surround herself with people who valued her for more than her résumé.

Even in those uncertain days, Aminatou didn't feel jealous of her friends who had stable jobs, because she felt so supported by them. Sure, she wasn't making any money or doing anything fulfilling, but at least she had a winning team around her. She knew that the gulf between what she was capable of and the opportunities she was offered would close one day. It was just taking way longer than she had expected. It wasn't like her friends had *their* dream jobs either.

Ann didn't care that Aminatou didn't have a high-powered DC job—or any job at all. She thought Aminatou was brilliant and impressive! We said "funemployed" to keep the mood light, but Aminatou still had to fight a feeling of foreboding. Ann was a sounding board for all of Aminatou's ideas about which professional path she would consider once this visa stuff was all cleared up, but there was only so much a friend could do. The immigration situation loomed like an oppressive cloud, and despite her lawyer's tireless work and optimism, Aminatou was convinced she would have to leave the country.

As her asylum claim made its way through the court system, Aminatou was granted a new work authorization—baby steps—and with the help of a friend who worked at a marketing firm, she was hired as an online analyst.

Aminatou had always wanted a job where she could effect

change on a large scale and reach a lot of people. She thought she'd be weighing in on bank bailouts and saving the country from economic collapse, but now instead she would be recapping online trends for Domino's Pizza, lurking on beauty message boards, and running a competition to help pick the next Gerber Baby, all while praying she didn't get assigned to work with the shady Republican client running for Congress. This was not her dream job, and she had to give herself a real attitude check about it. She tried to shake off the feeling that this was a step down for her, and lean into the fact that she would be learning about a new field. It sounds so old-timey and laughable now, but in the late 2000s, social media really upended certain professions. Some established people looked down on it, but Aminatou quickly realized it was an advantage to be good at something that puzzled her bosses and that they weren't willing to learn themselves. It meant *she* could be the expert.

Another major upside was that she was earning more than twice as much money as she had been making at the think tank—again, she negotiated for it—and she continued to ask for a raise any time she got a chance. Aminatou learned that if they give you what you ask for without flinching, you probably didn't ask for enough. She also started asking the men in her life how much *they* made, and she was appalled when she realized most of her women friends were grossly underpaid. These men weren't smarter or more talented. They just asked for more. And they usually got it. Aminatou knew this was a muscle she would have to exercise.

Ann's work situation was in flux too. She had been promoted to deputy editor and was excited when the magazine brought in a new editor in chief—one who really respected Ann's skills and opinions as his second in command. For a while, things were pretty good. But when that editor announced he was leaving, the magazine's founders told Ann that she would not be promoted to replace him. She knew she was only 29, but she'd seen young men with comparable experience given the opportunity to lead a magazine. She couldn't imagine sticking around—at the magazine or in this city—if there was little chance she could advance.

This realization would kick off a period, lasting from 2010 to 2016, during which one or both of us moved almost every year, crisscrossing the country in search of better job prospects. We were all over the place. When we hit a roadblock that we couldn't push through, we looked for a new path. Sometimes it was because we wanted to shift the focus of our careers. Sometimes it was because we wanted a salary bump or a better position, and we could see we were never going to get it from our current employer. The roadblocks weren't all in our minds. Years later we would read a report based on data from more than 600 companies, which found that women are less likely than men to be promoted internally. No wonder we both felt like we had to jump around in order to move up.

In Ann's case, she knew she needed a change—or several big ones, all at once. Although she loved being an editor, she had been saying since childhood that she wanted to be a writer. And even though she cared about politics, she was sick of editing extremely dry articles about disagreements within the labor movement and the finer points of foreign policy. She didn't see herself landing a staff-writing job. (Although we'll never know! She didn't apply for any.) So despite her frequent rants about sexism and ageism, she was ultimately OK with not getting the promotion to executive editor. If she was honest with herself, Ann didn't want to head into her 30s with a job that was going nowhere in a city she had never loved.

So she quit.

Even though her savings account was barely full enough to cover a snack run to Whole Foods, it seemed like the time to go freelance. "Self-employed" sounded even better than "funemployed," right? She had a small editing contract with her previous employer that would pay the rent for a while. Now that she could work from anywhere, she packed up her reliable Honda sedan and set off for Austin, Texas—a move that would cut her rent in half and get her out of DC.

It seems like this should have been a huge issue for our friendship. After all, Ann wouldn't just be leaving town; she would be leaving her chosen family. Aminatou could have been upset that Ann decided to move away. But Aminatou wholeheartedly supported the move because she understood what it represented for her friend. Ann had always been sour on DC, and Aminatou wanted her to be happy. She knew Ann would want the same for her but she still cried watching her drive away.

Just a few weeks into self-employment, Ann was already pushing down her money panic. She tried to focus on the positives—no bosses! working without a bra on!—but she couldn't envision how she'd make it work long-term without a staff job. Her bank statement was all debits and no credits.

Then a deus ex Gmail arrived. It was from the founder of a magazine in Los Angeles. Was Ann interested in applying for an executive editor position? Ann might have screamed when she read it. Or maybe she gasped. She doesn't remember. What's certain is that she immediately called Aminatou. This was huge. It was a position based in California, a place she'd always wanted to return to—even if it meant leaving Austin and her freelance experiment after only a month. A title like executive editor was a major step up. But it was more than that: it was Ann's chance to prove she could do this boss-level job better than all the people for whom she'd worked in the past. She was exhilarated and intimidated all at once. Like Aminatou, Ann was familiar with the frustration of underemployment, and she knew she was capable of so much more. She didn't want to blow this opportunity.

Ann had always relied on Aminatou not just as a close friend but as someone to turn to for professional advice and support. This job opportunity presented a whole new set of challenges, and from the moment the email arrived Ann was leaning on Aminatou harder than ever. After a quick call with her potential new employer, Ann learned that the job involved overseeing a million-dollar budget, developing a new editorial strategy, hiring a whole team of editors and writers, and, ultimately, being responsible for drawing thousands of new readers to the magazine. Her friends assured her that, duh, she could absolutely handle all of this—in fact, she was the perfect person for the job. (In retrospect, Ann was right to be concerned. This was six jobs folded into one!)

A week later Ann flew to Los Angeles for the interview, a day long series of meetings with every single person at the small company, without even a bathroom break. At one point the founder asked her to draw out an editorial org chart on a whiteboard in the meeting room, right there on the spot. By the end of the day, with sweat stains ringing the pits of her boss-lady silk blouse, Ann called Aminatou from her rental car in tears because she was sure she'd messed up and would never get a job offer. Even later that night, after her friend on staff told her that everyone had liked her, Ann didn't believe him.

A few days later, though, the offer arrived. Ann took a second to celebrate, then steeled herself. It was time to negotiate.

With the confidence of someone who's always reading business books and watching *Shark Tank*, Aminatou assured Ann that this new job was a six-figure level of responsibility. Plus Ann should get her moving costs covered, and maybe a signing bonus.

> **ANN:** i don't even know how to ask for a signing bonus!
>
> **AMINATOU:** girl i only recently started making over 35k. do we need to tweet suze orman for advice?

This is something that separates close friends from mentors or workplace confidantes. It wasn't that Ann viewed Aminatou as a guru who knew everything about the art of professional negotiation. What was important to Ann was Aminatou's presence with her in the confusion. In fact, Aminatou had only recently learned from her friend Antoine what a moving bonus even was.

> **ANTOINE:** ask for twice as much. They'll say no if they can't afford it. Oh also ask for a moving bonus!
>
> **AMINATOU:** a bonus for moving??? THAT IS A THING?? How come men just feel entitled to all this stuff we are too shy to ask for. MERCI BB

Ann decided, with Aminatou and her other friends cheering her on, that she would ask for the unimaginable annual salary of . . . *[RuPaul voice]* $100,000. Aminatou couldn't keep a straight face whenever we said the number out loud, but she was proud of Ann for asking for her worth. The next day Ann emailed Aminatou and the other friends who had been helping her strategize:

> *i just accepted the job. i fought for the $100k salary and got it (plus $2500 for moving costs and a $10k bonus if i meet traffic goals).*
>
> *i start april 1. i never ever could have done it without you. !!!*
>
> *love,*
> *Ann Friedman*
> *Executive Editor*

What a nerd.

Then a whole new type of panic set it: not whether she would get the job, not how much she would be paid for it, but whether she was actually able to do it well. *What if I fail?* The question was always lurking in the back of her mind. But Ann got to work making budgets and hiring plans, falling asleep every night with her laptop in bed.

As Ann learned how to cosplay "confident, capable top-level boss," Aminatou's advice was invaluable. When we were out of our depth, Aminatou would recite our mantra: fake it till you make it. Ann had *years* to perfect the arts of budgeting and hiring. What was important now was to keep pushing forward and just do her best. Ann knew that on paper she was qualified for the new job. And she knew she could actually do it in practice because her friends would be alongside her every step of the way.

"I could never do it without you!" Ann wailed in gratitude.

"I don't shine if you don't shine," Aminatou told her.

Eventually we started calling this Shine Theory.

Even before we used the words "Shine Theory," it was an operating principle of our friendship. We came to define Shine Theory as an investment, over the long term, in helping a friend be their best—and relying on their help in return. It is a conscious decision to bring our full selves to our friendships and to not let insecurity or envy ravage them. It's a practice of cultivating a spirit of genuine happiness and excitement when our friends are doing well, and being there for them when they aren't.

Shine Theory is part of the reason Aminatou supported Ann's decision to move away from DC. It's why Ann was by Aminatou's side every step of the way as she figured out her visa situation. We wanted the best for each other. Every time a friend has encouraged us to follow through with a life change we've been talking about forever, or gently pushed us to get a therapist, or supported us in leaving a dead-end job, they were practicing Shine Theory. They wanted us to shine our brightest. And often, wanting the best for our friends has prompted us to seek better things for ourselves too.

Shine Theory can be applied to any arena of life where our

ambitions lie, from the domestic to the professional. It's when we care deeply about achieving a goal—getting a promotion, having a family, mastering a skill—that we often default to feeling competitive. We start to view the world as a series of power rankings. Shine Theory asks that we replace that impulse of competition with one of collaboration.

One of the clearest ways to see Shine Theory in action is to look at the work world. After years of watching our male peers get priority boarding on the professional rocket ship while we were on standby in the gate area, we stopped internalizing this as a personal failure. Together, we became skeptical of gatekeepers and decided we'd get further if we helped each other. We pooled our contacts and resources, affirmed each other when we felt stymied by bosses who didn't see our value, and strategized together to get the highest salary possible. We brought bridal-shower levels of energy to news of a friend's promotion and greeted pay raises with high-pitched squeals of joy.

Shine Theory is especially useful for people who don't look like the traditional power players in their industry. There has long been a sense among marginalized folks, if only at a subconscious level, that there are a limited number of spaces for us at the top. Have you ever seen a voting ballot that's more than 50 percent female? Or a Fortune 500 boardroom packed with people of color? This lack of representation has created a pervasive scarcity mentality: the idea that there are only a few great jobs and you have to compete with people who look like you to get one of them.

Within our own friendship, it's not an exaggeration to say that we've never felt an ounce of professional jealousy. Granted, we have always had different career goals and never applied for the same job—which certainly made it easier. But we like to think that our support for each other would have remained steadfast even if we had. We know we'll rise faster, go further, and have more fun if we do it together.

This isn't really a radical idea. In fact, it's at the foundation of many long-standing systems. The organizing principle of expensive private schools, for example, is that powerful people get more powerful by building close bonds with each other over several decades. That's what the proverbial old boys' club is all about too. It's not who you are; it's who you know. We take that idea and apply it to sharing power, not hoarding it.

No matter the arena we're practicing it in, Shine Theory starts with refusing to give in to comparison and competition, and trying instead to forge a bond and a connection. When we notice a person seems to have something we want, instead of turning them into an external barometer for how we're feeling about ourselves, we work to see them as a potential ally. We have come to realize that if someone is tearing us down or targeting us as competition, it's often because they are lacking in confidence or support themselves. We try to be the one to take the first step and declare that we are willing to work hard to collaborate. We try to consider how far we could get together.

Notice we say "try." This can be hard sometimes, especially when you're early in your career and feel like you need to hold tight to the few opportunities and connections you have. Ann can easily recall the spike of jealousy she felt, back when she was toiling at her desk as a fact-checking intern, when she saw that a woman her age had written a *New York Times Magazine* cover story. *What does she have that I don't?* Ann fumed to herself. How had this woman gotten such a plum assignment, while Ann was still paying her dues and checking other writers' facts?

An older and wiser Ann would counsel her younger self to find an email address for the cover-story writer, congratulate her, and just *ask* her how she did it. That would have been one way to turn a minor fit of pique into a positive professional alliance. Even if she didn't end up befriending the other young woman, at least Ann might have had more information about how her industry worked—which would have been really valuable at a time in her career when she had few contacts and no inside knowledge. Who knows? She and that woman may have even become friends.

The world is not a game with one winner and the rest losers. But in a few specific situations, it *is* zero-sum. Sometimes we *have* been in direct competition with someone we'd rather consider a collaborator. Aminatou was once passed over for a promotion that went to a young woman she didn't always agree with. Their positions at the company often put them at odds with each other on how best to use resources, and they had very different working styles. In the sexist version of this movie, they would have been muttering, "What a bitch," after every meeting. In reality, they found a way to work with each other, and when this woman was later promoted again, she advocated for Aminatou to fill her previous position. You can want to be picked for a position or promoted over someone else and still be an adherent of Shine Theory—as long as you keep things in perspective.

It's not a failure of Shine Theory to feel a twinge of jealousy or envy sometimes, but it's how you act on those feelings that matters. Even if you don't forge a lifelong supportive bond with every person you meet or hear about—and you probably won't—Shine

Theory can help you move on so you're not just stewing in your own resentment.

Some people will have you believe that by sharing the knowledge you've gained, you are losing your advantage. It's simply not true. Shine Theory has only moved us closer to our goals. We have gained so much by sharing information that helped our friends get new jobs, make more money, or navigate tricky work problems. The researcher Adam Grant has found that the people who are unafraid to share their knowledge and resources with others in their community are the most likely to succeed over the long term.

And make no mistake, Shine Theory is a long game. At the start of our careers, it was mainly about commiserating and strategizing a way through our problems when we didn't have much power or many resources. Now that we're older and more established, we still don't have all the answers. But we have gained more connections, experience, and financial security—which means we're able to help each other in more meaningful ways. We're in a position to support each other even more.

Shine Theory hasn't neutered our ambition—quite the opposite. We are two women who run only if something's on fire, but we hope to follow the example of the distance runner Shalane Flanagan. After she won the 2017 New York City Marathon, it was reported that she had been training 11 other women runners. This is because Flanagan saw a need. There was no community of women distance runners, who tended to burst on the scene after college and then burn out quickly. As one of the few women in her sport with staying power, Flanagan could have enjoyed her solo elite status. Instead, she got to work helping her potential competitors, offering everything from training tips to pep talks. Every single one of them has since made it to the Olympics. The *New York Times* called it "the Shalane Effect." Flanagan created a cohort and became a better runner herself because of it. She proves that you can be hypercompetitive and at the top of your game, and still be an incredible supporter and collaborator. The payoff is huge. "When we achieve great things on our own, it doesn't feel nearly as special," she told the *Times*.

Flanagan is also a great example of why Shine Theory goes deeper than mere networking. She could have patted those other runners on the back and told them "good luck" and gone on to join a running group with men—the equivalent of exchanging email addresses at an awkward professional conference and never following up. Instead, she made a real investment of her time and knowledge. Shine Theory is not about collecting contact info or trying to help every single person we meet along the way, because if we're doing it right, it's simply not possible to invest deeply in that many people. That's why we always specify that Shine Theory is mutual, meaningful investment, over the long term.

One of the most fulfilling things about our relationship is the fact that it has pushed us to grow and be better humans. We're not alone in enjoying this facet of friendship. A Northwestern University study showed that people prefer to make friends with other people who can help them achieve their goals. At the same time, they're not even aware that that's something they're selecting for. Seeing something in your friend that you want to achieve yourself can help you get closer to who you want to be. We're pretty sure this is part of the spark we felt on the very first night we met.

A successful woman whom Aminatou deeply admires once gave her a piece of advice she has taken to heart: At the moments when you're leveling up—say, you're accepting a promotion or you're on an extravagant vacation you can finally afford or you're at the Grammys—take a look at who is surrounding you. You cannot be surrounded by people you've known for only two years.

It was an exhortation to bring your people along for the ride. The people who know where you come from. The people who know what values you hold. The people who give you the gut checks you need. These are the people who will help you make the best decisions with the power and resources you have. They are also the people with whom you will want to enjoy your newfound success. This is why we have always loved the show *Entourage*, despite the shitty bro behavior. We love watching people glow up together.

We call it a theory, but really it's a practice. It's not just something we say. It's something we do.

Shine Theory often takes the form of sharing resources, contacts, and opportunities. One of the most helpful things we can do for someone is connect them to someone else. Aminatou found the job that allowed her to stay in the United States thanks to some crucial inside info from a friend. And Ann got her dream job in Los Angeles only because a friend put forth her name. If we turn down an opportunity, we make a point of recommending someone else in our network. And if we have the bandwidth, we try to be intentional about getting our peers together to talk about what's happening in their careers. Ann and another young editor used to host a happy hour for women journalists in DC; Aminatou and a friend started an email list for women in technology to guide one another through job searches and technical problems. We both practice "ask and offer," a tactic introduced to us by Pipeline Angels founder Natalia Oberti Noguera that pushes us to be concrete about what we need and to articulate what we can provide in return. It helps remove the stigma of asking for help, and it forces us to reflect on all the knowledge we have to share.

Shine Theory also goes hand in hand with transparency, because it's impossible to level up if you don't have a sense of where you rank. There was a whole Supreme Court case fought about this. It was brought by Lilly Ledbetter, who worked the night shift at Goodyear Tire & Rubber Company for almost 20 years. One day, an anonymous coworker slipped a note into her mailbox, alerting her to the fact that three of her male coworkers were doing the same job she was but being paid $1,000 more each month. Ledbetter was outraged. (Can you imagine being in your 60s and finding out you've been systematically underpaid for decades? You would be burning with rage too.) When she filed a complaint, her bosses retaliated by assigning her to a more physically demanding job. That didn't stop her, and she took her case all the way to the Supreme Court, which ruled in 2007 that Ledbetter had filed her discrimination complaint too late and could not receive damages from her employer. She didn't let that stop her either. Despite the Supreme Court decision, she kept telling her story to politicians and eventually testified in front of Congress. The first bill that President Obama signed into law was the Lilly Ledbetter Fair Pay Act, which makes it easier for employees to challenge pay discrimination in court. When we share salary information, we do so with deep gratitude for people like Lilly Ledbetter and her anonymous note-writer, who taught us how important it is to practice transparency.

Shine Theory can also take the form of a warning. Decades before "me too" became a widespread shorthand for making abuse and harassment public, people would quietly share with each other the identities of men who had a tendency to abuse their power. Ann used to have an elaborate inside "joke" with a few other women in media. It was called "The Island," and the narrative went like this: All the editors and writers known to be sexual harassers or professional bullies are on a flight together, probably heading to some sort of "ideas festival," when the plane goes down on a small island. (Ann's bullying boss from San Francisco is definitely on the flight manifest.) There, they are forced to live out the rest of their days with only one another to harass. With them out of the picture, Ann and her colleagues are free to remake their industry into a creative, forward-thinking, equitable paradise.

It was satisfying to picture this scenario but also a sad coping mechanism. The people who told this "joke" believed these men were too professionally powerful, too entrenched to really be held accountable for their behavior.

Years later, Ann and her colleagues were proven wrong when several of these men were removed from their jobs after they were outed for making crude comments around the office or watching porn on their work computers or even assaulting their colleagues. But before the "me too" reckoning, when no one powerful enough to fire these men seemed to give a shit, The Island was an important code for women to tell each other which men sincerely wanted to be mentors, which ones were dangerous, and which ones were somewhere in between, seeking the thrill of having a cocktail under the guise of professionalism. "Is he on The Island or not?" Ann and her colleagues asked each other. Or they'd warn, "Watch out, that guy's totally on The Island." This too was a form of Shine Theory.

Sometimes Shine Theory looks like helping each other be heard. In the early days of the Obama administration, two-thirds of the president's top aides were men. Alyssa Mastromonaco, a former advisor to President Obama, told us that it is prestigious and advantageous to be in a meeting with the president. If you are able to say, "I was in the Oval today and Barack Obama asked me my opinion," she said, "that shit pays dividends for a hundred years." She and other women soon noticed that in meetings with the president, a lot of men had no qualms about sitting front and center at the table. Meanwhile, the more reticent women on staff tended to hang back in the wings, even though some of them were way more essential to the meeting. The women began encouraging one another to sit front and center and to speak up. "The more confident you feel, the more you feel like you pay it forward to other people," Mastromonaco says.

The women on staff also devised a strategy they called "amplification": if one woman spoke up, another would repeat her point and make sure to say her name to give credit where credit was due. President Obama noticed and began making more of a point to call on women at the table. The women got themselves heard because they formed a strategic, united front.

Once you know what it looks like, you'll see Shine Theory everywhere.

A fter we began using Shine Theory as a private shorthand, Ann wrote a column that introduced the concept to the world. At the time, we didn't really think of it as a formal debut. Neither of us knew it would take on a life of its own. But this column was a viral hit.

Aminatou had an uneasy feeling about the fact that something she had shared with Ann privately was up for consumption by the whole world. She was now a professional marketer, and she knew that after things start circulating online, they can quickly lose their context and, sometimes, their meaning. She also knew that retaining ownership of your ideas can be a real mess if you don't have a plan.

We had no such plan.

Shine Theory was getting a lot of traction as a hashtag. People were using it to describe relationships in their own lives and applying it to prominent examples they saw in the news. This was our first clue that it was resonating with so many more people than us. When we went to buy the domain name, we were astonished to find out that someone else was already using shinetheory.com. And it gets worse: it was a gross fitness website aimed at women, with the word "TRADEMARK" prominently displayed across it. Everything about it made us recoil. This person was not only stealing our idea; they had also filed paperwork to claim it as their own. We won't bore you with the details, but after thousands of dollars in legal and filing fees we definitely couldn't afford, the trademark, URL, and social-media handles for Shine Theory all belonged to us.

We were right to be so protective. As the public conversation about Shine Theory unfolded over the next few years, it was clear some people really understood our description of mutual investment. But others were eager to use it as an easy shorthand for "women's empowerment," feminism's terrible stepsister that helps sell everything from period underwear to leadership conferences without actually challenging the way businesses and governments operate. More than one tech company tried to brand their women's history month effort as Shine Theory. Someone gave a TEDx Talk devoted to it. An Instagram platform for "creatives" used Shine Theory as a theme for their sponsored content, selling ads against it. We are not above a networking event, but we hated seeing Shine Theory distorted to the point where the commitment and personal risk were stripped out.

But we've also gotten dozens of emails from teachers and Girl Scout leaders who use the concept in their lesson plans. We never tire of seeing social-media posts in which a friend celebrates her friend's success. Anywhere you can find a group of people who are working together to advance their individual and collective goals, you won't be surprised to hear a Shine Theory reference. Especially when the people in question have been historically shut out of the halls of power.

That includes the literal halls of power. In 2018, 24 women who had never served in Congress before were elected to the House of Representatives. In the first days of the 116th Congress, many of these new leaders took to the internet to express support and admiration for one another. And they made it clear from the start that they would be working as a team. Alexandria Ocasio-Cortez, a representative from New York, tweeted that she was "so incredibly proud" of Ayanna Pressley, Massachusetts's first African-American congresswoman. In response, Pressley thanked Ocasio-Cortez for "living #shinetheory out loud."

This is such a powerful example because, despite how cozy these women were making it look, politics is another cutthroat sport. Members of Congress are competing for national media attention and plum committee assignments, as well as resources for their constituents (appropriations, baby!). Instead of cutting each other down, hoarding their power, or hogging the spotlight, the congresswomen were signaling that they were indeed friends. Ilhan Omar, a representative from Minnesota and the first Somali American elected to Congress, has called Ocasio-Cortez her "partner in justice." In an interview about how this group of new congresswomen had been early in calling for an impeachment inquiry into President Trump, Omar said, "I think he is terrified by any women who are practicing Shine Theory, who have each other's back."

They understood. Shine Theory is intentional. It is accountable. It is personal. And you have to actually put in the work.

FIVE

The Stretch

I t started with a mysterious missing tampon.

Aminatou had started a new job at a PR firm in DC and needed to be up earlier than usual to monitor the news and assist with her clients' live TV appearances. It was a fast-paced job, and as someone whose brain doesn't really wake up until after lunch, she felt like she might break at any moment. Her body also was not cooperating. She had always had incredibly painful and heavy periods, but they were getting worse. She chalked it up to work stress. On this day, the bleeding was even more intense than usual. When she went to the bathroom to change her tampon, she couldn't find it. The one that was supposed to be in her vagina, that is. At first she was puzzled and then panic set in. *What if it's lost?*

News flash: you cannot lose a tampon so far up inside your

body that it's gone forever. (That's why Goddess created the cervix.) But that day in the office bathroom, all of her exhaustion seemed to hit her at once. She started crying. What was *wrong* with her? Aminatou pulled down her American Apparel miniskirt (RIP), went back to her desk, and made an appointment with the first gynecologist who could fit her in. She wished Ann was nearby to help quell her panic, but text messages would have to do.

A few hours later Aminatou was in an exam room nervously fidgeting in her gown when the doctor walked in. In a thick Ukrainian accent, the gynecologist started the medical exam with a barrage of statements and questions. "You are very pale," she said, barely looking up from her position between the stirrups. Aminatou already knew this. It's very alarming to look in the mirror as a Black person and understand that you look pale—more than the routine ashiness that can happen to anyone who's not moisturized enough. There seemed to be no color on her skin or in her eyelids lately—or, apparently, in her vagina.

The pelvic exam didn't turn up a runaway tampon, but the doctor was concerned at how much bleeding Aminatou was experiencing and recommended that she get back on birth control to regulate her periods. Aminatou felt a sense of relief. At last, a professional had confirmed something was in fact wrong with her, but she was still very tired. You know that feeling when you're trying to walk out of the ocean and the waves just keep pulling you back into the water, and you feel like you're not moving at all even though you're exerting all the effort you can muster? That was how she felt half of the time. The other half of the time she felt like the beach itself, full of wet sand. No amount of rest or sleep was refreshing. As she sat in the doctor's office, she wondered how she would even begin to explain her health situation to her boss. This wasn't like the flu or a broken bone. There was no straightforward reason for her to stay home in bed. She decided she would have to just push through it.

Aminatou was scheduled to travel to New York the following week to give a work presentation, and the thought of being far away from home and bleeding this profusely was making her even more anxious than usual. The doctor ordered some tests and sent Aminatou off with a prescription for birth control, telling her that would reduce the bleeding.

Aminatou was on her work trip—about to stand up and give her presentation, in fact—when her doctor called. She heard a panicked Ukrainian-accented voice: "Where are you right now? I need you to get to the ER *right away*, Aminatou." The doctor made her write down some test numbers and insisted she find the nearest emergency room. Aminatou hung up, did her presentation, and then headed to a hospital a few blocks away. She called Mercedes, one of her closest friends from college who lived in Brooklyn, to let her know where she was but asked her not to worry. Mercedes immediately hopped in a car and soon showed up with magazines and snacks.

Meanwhile Ann, thousands of miles away in Los Angeles, frantically texted Mercedes for updates. She knew that Aminatou had not been feeling well, but this turn of events was alarming. Ann hated how helpless she felt, and desperately wished she was a cab ride away from the hospital.

The doctors ran more blood work, and a verdict came very swiftly. It was iron-deficiency anemia. The symptoms were all adding up: the brain fog, the exhaustion, the paleness, the leg cramps, the insomnia. This type of anemia, the doctors told her, is very common during pregnancy or in people with heavy menstrual periods. The heavy flow was apparently the culprit. Based on Aminatou's hemoglobin numbers, one of the ER doctors said he would have expected her to be passed out somewhere, which also explained why her gynecologist had been so worried. Something was *very* wrong.

After a blood transfusion Aminatou felt brand-new. The fog cleared from her brain, and she no longer felt like her body was made of wet sand. She could walk without getting headaches. The color returned to her skin. Aminatou slept in Mercedes' bed that night, calmed by the belief that everything would get better now that she had a diagnosis.

In fact it was only a partial diagnosis. Doctors had figured out her heavy periods were the source of the anemia problem—and anemia explained why she was so tired all the time—but they couldn't figure out *why* Aminatou was bleeding so much every month. A few weeks later, she ended up at the emergency room again. Soon she was getting a blood transfusion every couple of months.

Chronic illness was Aminatou's new reality.

Her life was now divided between Good Days and Bad Days. The Bad Days came without warning and disrupted everything. She couldn't get out of bed. She was too exhausted to take a shower or pick up the paper from her stoop. She couldn't muster the energy for game nights, happy hours, or even the weddings of dear friends. Aminatou didn't think of herself as a flake, but lately she didn't seem to have a choice. She found herself waiting until the last possible minute to see if she could handle leaving the house, then realizing she couldn't. Whenever she pushed herself to go outside, it always ended in a cloud of fatigue and tears.

She was tired of not having a clear medical explanation for a condition that felt serious enough that she was missing significant life events. She was tired of talking to doctors who seemed just as puzzled as she was. She was tired of talking about how tired she was.

Ann was starting to see her fray at the edges. Aminatou tried to keep her up-to-date about what was going on with her body, but that felt impossible when she herself didn't quite understand.

And Ann was not the only one checking in, over and over, about the details of her condition. Before Aminatou knew it, she was fielding questions from many friends. Her entire medical history was on the table for discussion. If she had said, "I don't feel well, I have a cold," everyone would have understood that and not pried further. But she didn't have a cold. She needed to have multiple procedures—often involving very intimate parts of her body—and her friends always had follow-up questions. She did not want to share every excruciating detail. Aminatou wanted some privacy.

At the same time, she was afraid her friends would get bored of asking her how she was doing and eventually vanish from her life. The more time that passed without a concrete diagnosis, the more Aminatou retreated inward. She didn't want anyone's pity, and she didn't want to be a burden to her friends. It was a painful spiral. She had a string of Bad Days, she got depressed about it, she pushed everyone away, they worried and reached out, so she would push them further away. Rinse and repeat.

But she never had to feel guilty about canceling plans with

long-distance friends like Ann. Thanks to digital contact, Aminatou could be present without leaving the comfort of her couch.

We were still pretty new at the whole long-distance thing, but mostly we'd weathered the change. We had regular video-chat dates. (Ann actually upgraded her ancient PC laptop to a newer Mac with a built-in camera for the express purpose of hanging out digitally with Aminatou.) We texted constantly. And every few months, whenever we had a wedding or work trip on the opposite coast, we would tack on a few days to see each other. We missed our long, unplanned weeknight hangs, but fundamentally, it didn't feel like too much had changed between us.

That is, until Aminatou got sick. As Aminatou started to have more and more Bad Days, being far away was starting to stress *Ann* out. She didn't want to pry, but she was often unsure about what was going on with Aminatou's health or how she was really feeling. Ann was a lot better at assessing her friend's emotional state in person. Mediated by the phone or the computer, she wasn't as sure.

> **AMINATOU:** and ok now let me tell you what taking 4 birth control pills does to you.
> **AMINATOU:** [REDACTED]
> **ANN:** hahahahahaha. Amina.
> **AMINATOU:** [REDACTED]
> **ANN:** i am laughing so hard
> **AMINATOU:** this is my life
> **ANN:** OHMYGOD
> **ANN:** WHEN are we vidchatting? i miss you so much. cannot handle.

Ann loved Aminatou's jokes (which we've had to redact to protect the innocent), but she also knew that humor was one of Aminatou's deflection techniques when she was worried or anxious. Ann laughed along and then tried to push these conversations to video chat, so she could get a look at Aminatou's face and try to gauge how she was *really* doing. Sometimes she succeeded.

Mostly, though, Ann was at a loss. Ann could send texts to check in on days when she knew Aminatou had a doctor's appointment, and Ann could send anemia-busting care packages of beef jerky and iron-rich paleo snacks. But the kind of support Aminatou needed often required an in-person friend who could knock on her door to check in, just hang out with her at home, or accompany her to the doctor. These were things Ann couldn't do from the other coast, and she worried about Aminatou constantly. At the same time, she didn't want to make illness the only thing she ever asked about. So Ann would often check in with mutual friends to get a sense of how things were going. She had never been more grateful to have so many friends in common—and at the same time felt guilty, because checking up on Aminatou was also talking about her behind her back. Ann knew how important Aminatou's privacy was to her.

We thought the physical distance between us was no big deal, but chronic illness was proving us wrong. We were starting to feel stretched.

Hang in here with us while we struggle to recall a few things we learned in PE. (Or, rather, a few things *Aminatou* learned in PE. Ann learned only shame and bitterness in gym class.) When it comes to exercise, you probably already understand the importance of stretching. Even those of us who would rather sit at home and watch HGTV than lace up our sneakers understand that it's not enough to bulk up or become an aerobics master. You have to be flexible too. And in order to become flexible, you have to stretch. All the time, in fact.

Stretching keeps your muscles strong and healthy, and you need that flexibility to maintain a range of motion. Without it, the muscles shorten and become tight. Then, when you call on the muscles for activity (god forbid you decide to actually go jogging), they are weak and unable to extend all the way. That means pain and damage. Stretching immediately before any physical activity won't magically give you perfect flexibility. You'll need to do it over time and remain committed to the process. (This is expensive advice we are recycling from physical therapy. You're welcome.)

The same principle applies to friendship. Stretching is the best metaphor we've come up with to describe all the ways our friends expand our world, challenge us, and inspire us to change. This give-and-take is necessary from the very beginning because no two people are exactly alike. Life inevitably brings changes. And those changes often shift the foundation on which the friendship was built. That's just how it is. You are not the person you were 10 years ago, and you won't be the exact same person in the next decade. For a Big Friendship to survive, it has to adapt.

There are little stretches that crop up early, like getting over the fact that it always takes your friend a full day to text you back or admitting that you don't like the same music. And there are slightly bigger stretches, which often present themselves later.

Maybe you used to live in the same neighborhood, and now that you live farther apart you have to decide whose turf you're going to meet on. Or bigger stretches, like you used to feel like financial equals, then one of you started making a *lot* more money, and suddenly things are tense every time the check comes. Then there are huge stretches, like renegotiating the terms of your friendship when one of you moves away or becomes a parent—or develops a chronic illness. You could go years with a friendship requiring only a comfortable, familiar set of stretches, and then one of you starts working a night shift, becomes a primary caregiver, or meets their future spouse, and you have to learn a whole new repertoire.

A healthy friendship involves stretches in both directions. When you're stretching, you're both making an effort to figure out how to adapt to your differences and to the shifting shape of your bond. Just like exercise, some of this emotional stretching feels good, and some of it will make you feel like you can't take it anymore. Stretching is being challenged, in a way that is both difficult and rewarding at the same time. The amount of stretching doesn't have to feel equal in every single moment—sometimes one person will require more from the friendship than the other—but over time, the *give* has to even out with the *take*.

Sometimes stretching comes effortlessly. We call it a passive stretch: you just do it, without even thinking about it. You happen to both pick up a hobby at the same time. Or you find yourself with encyclopedic knowledge of Céline Dion, just because your friend is a huge fan, even though you've never been one for power ballads. Or you easily adopt a new routine when one of you breaks your foot and can no longer meet up for daily walks.

But most stretches, especially ones related to life changes, are active: You make video-chat dates with your friend after they move 3,000 miles away rather than expecting them to show up on your doorstep in a pair of sweatpants. You push yourself to talk about a specific way your friend hurt your feelings, even though you're scared to bring it up. After one of you becomes a parent or gets a time-consuming job, you figure out how to maintain the friendship with fewer hours to devote to each other. An active stretch can feel so challenging you're not sure that you will be able to sustain it.

This was the kind of stretch that Aminatou's chronic illness demanded of her. Asking for support is a very big stretch for Aminatou. People always offer, and of course that comes from a good place. But in the past, she has accepted help and been let down when the promised support never showed up, which made it hard for her to ask again. On a deeper level, asking for help is admitting vulnerability—not an easy thing for an extremely independent person. Aminatou has had to learn not to wince whenever a friend offers her a well-meaning but vague " What can I do?" Sometimes the answer is really "Nothing, unless you're a doctor," and people can have a hard time hearing that. It's also been a stretch to have conversations with friends who say they understand she cannot hang out, but then express disappointment that she can't.

Ann was stretched by Aminatou's illness in her own way. She had to find ways of staying up-to-date on her friend's health without crossing Aminatou's privacy boundaries. Ann had to figure out how to keep showing up for her friend, without the benefit of being able to drop by her house. And Ann had to forge closer bonds with some of Aminatou's friends who she didn't know well, because of their shared interest in making sure Aminatou was doing OK.

One reason this stretch was even possible is that Ann already had some experience with it. Her biggest and earliest stretch involved a different friendship and a different chronic illness. When Ann's closest high-school friend, Bridget, started feeling depressed, they were in their early teen years—a nightmarish time even if you aren't dealing with a mental-health crisis. And Bridget was really suffering. A diagnosis of chronic depression and a Prozac prescription seemed to help and hurt in equal measure. Ann had no experience with mental illness, but she was the only person who knew how bad things had gotten for her best friend.

Even though it was a stretch to understand everything her friend was going through, Ann spent hours with Bridget in their respective bedrooms and kept in constant communication with her (as much as pre-smartphone friendship allowed). They shared every emotion and most hours of the day when they weren't separated by their class schedule at school. In fact, they were so close that it would have been harder for Bridget to *hide* what she was going through than to share it with Ann. It forced Bridget to be more open about her illness and her needs than she otherwise would have.

"Now when I need to communicate with people about what I'm going through or the needs I have, I think about high school all the time," Bridget told Ann many years later. "I think about how I would communicate it to you, or what you would say back to me. I guess the things you said to me in high school have always stuck with me. That's really when I learned how to share it with someone else rather than hide it."

That's how Ann learned how to keep showing up for a friend with chronic illness. She had learned to stretch for Bridget, so she was able to stretch for Aminatou. Over time, Aminatou was also learning how to stretch to stay in her friends' lives. She had to, because a chronic illness is, by definition, one with no end in sight.

Even if it got easier, we were both going to have to keep stretching. Indefinitely.

If the concept of stretching challenges you, that's normal. Most of us don't like to venture too far out of our comfort zones, especially when it comes to friendship, which we've been taught is supposed to always feel easy and harmonious. For the two of us, stretching is challenging because we think of ourselves as competent people, and we are afraid of looking foolish or failing as we try a stretch and realize we're not flexible enough to complete it. Sometimes we worry that our friend won't stretch as much as we are. Ultimately, we are creatures of comfort who don't like to be unsettled. These are all the same reasons Ann has had to psych herself up for every yoga class she's ever taken, and Aminatou hasn't signed up for a half marathon.

Sometimes the challenge of navigating difference in friendship goes beyond stretching. It feels like a strain. It can be hard to tell the difference between stretch and strain. If one person in the friendship is consistently stretched more than the other—adapting to the other person's needs, or always having to explain herself and feeling like the other person isn't retaining anything—it's probably more of a strain than a stretch. When two people aren't stretching at the same rate or with the same level of generosity, when one person consistently takes more than they give, the friendship starts to pull apart.

One-way stretch problems can be a hard thing to identify in real time, because everything can't feel equal in *every* moment. "When someone's asking too much of us, maybe we make the sacrifice because that's what our friend needs," says Jordan Pickell, a therapist in private practice in Vancouver. But she cautions that it's important to pay attention to feelings of anger, resentment, or frustration, which can be a signal that you're being stretched beyond your capacity. "That needs to be communicated, because it's no longer feeling like a mutually caring and respectful relationship." A healthy friendship, Pickell continues, is one "where people are bringing their true feelings and needs into the relationship."

Even though we were both stretching for each other to account for distance and illness, the "true feelings" part is where we weren't doing so great. We were stretching but couldn't always share our feelings about the stretch in real time. This would come back to bite us later. But at least we both recognized that a stretch was necessary, and did our best to complete it.

It can be extremely hard to figure out the right amount of growth and sacrifice to be devoting to a friendship, because we're not taught that friends are worth stretching for at all. Your spouse? Definitely, you'll need to work hard to adapt and change together—just consult one of the dozens of advice books out there or get a couples therapist. Your family? There's a therapist for that too. Friends, though? When things get hard, it's socially acceptable to abandon them with no conversation about it what-soever, even if you've been intimate parts of each other's lives for years. You're fully empowered to cut them out of your life.

What's a friendship that's worth stretching for? How each friend answers that question often determines which friendships fail and which get stronger. Until we posed this question to our-selves, we had never once considered how we decide to stretch for a friend. And upon reflection, it's clear we haven't always handled our stretching dilemmas gracefully.

For Aminatou, it's impossible to say whether a friendship is worth it until she's fully completed the stretch—or not. Either she finds herself doing the work, or she doesn't. If a stretch feels fun, thrilling, or emotionally low stakes, she's all about it. Aminatou will say yes to *any* adventurous trip that a friend wants to take or an activity they want to rope her into. But if a friendship is challenging her with discomfort and the pleasure reward is not tangible—if the stretch involves having a hard conversation, for example—for a long time, Aminatou was more likely to walk away from it and only realize later that she wrote off the friend-ship as not worth stretching for.

Ann agrees that some stretches are easy to identify as worth-while. She loves being pushed to rethink certain books or movies because her friends disagree with her about them. When deeper stretches are required, though, because things are getting uncom-fortable, Ann will sometimes decide not to make the effort. If she feels like she's been putting way more into a friendship than the other person, and she doesn't see that shifting any time soon, she simply stops stretching and waits for the other person to stretch back. If they never do, she doesn't lose sleep over it. The longer she's been friends with someone, the more she'll stretch without reciprocity. But even that has its limits. For Ann, deciding not to stretch usually ends up feeling like a slow fade, not a clean break—which is the kind of ghosting that can make former friends feel rejected and gaslit.

For friends, you don't *have* to stretch. You can choose to let the friendship break—and people do. All the time. If a friendship is still in its earliest days, difficult stretches are more likely to cause it to snap. You haven't developed the will to make sacrifices for each other yet. You can still picture what your lives would look like without the friendship. But if you consider each other chosen family, if you're practicing Shine Theory together, if you want to be in each other's lives for a very long time, then your friendship is probably big enough to stretch for. When one of you moves away or gets pregnant or gains a new partner or transitions (or insert your own significant life change here), the stakes are high. If you don't go through the shift together, it puts your friendship in jeopardy.

What's so maddening about friendship is that you don't always figure out simultaneously that a stretch is necessary. Sometimes one of you is stretched to the point of strain while the other friend doesn't even realize it. When you're not the one who's feeling stretched, it can be hard to notice all the effort your friend is putting in to sustain the friendship.

Other times *neither* of you realizes you should be stretching. It feels like there is no strife in the friendship, no disconnect at all. The ease of having been so close to each other for so long can actually create a threat because so much goes unsaid, so much is assumed. It's easy to forget that we're all changing constantly. We think this is why a lot of friendships don't survive big life transitions. If you can't acknowledge it openly when new circumstances are affecting your friendship, you can't stretch to account for them. There's a common shorthand for this: "We grew apart." Humans inevitably do change, and it's only natural that every friendship will not weather every shift.

Honestly, stretching rarely sounds appealing. If you're not already limber, it's likely to be painful or, at the very least, uncomfortable. But in a Big Friendship, both people make a conscious decision, often over and over again, that they're going to stretch toward each other. They might feel challenged but decide *not* to walk away. In fact, they will likely come to see their stretching as a necessary part of being in the friendship, a way of adapting to the inevitable changes that life contains.

It's only through deciding to stretch that we become stronger and grow. There is really no way around that. When we have stretched ourselves, it's not always fun in real time. But when we look back, we can see that it was our challenges, not our comforts, that have made us stronger, wiser, and more resilient.

SIX

..

The Friendweb

The first time we visited Austin together, about a year into our friendship, Aminatou arranged a group karaoke night. The email invitation said, "There is so little time and so many memories to make." She knew!

In the dank basement dive bar (love you, Ego's), Ann met Aminatou's warm, hilarious group of college friends in person. Brittany was like every glue-gun-owning Midwest diva she loved, but with a Texas twist. Lesley had the quickest wit in the state. Anna had her doubled over laughing. Ryan taught her to two-step. And Aminatou's friends met Ann's bestie Lara, who was also in town. It was one of those magical nights out. Duets were sung. Tequila was shot. Way too many photos were taken. As Lesley put it in a later email, "An Amina-endorsement is the highest honor in the land. The gods want this for us."

One reason the conversation flowed so easily is that this wasn't a meeting of strangers. Our friend groups were loosely knit together already thanks to the internet. We first got to know each other's long-distance friends in the comments on shared Google Reader posts, a mode of social media that is long dead, though we miss it every day. Basically, Google Reader was a private social-media feed. You could share posts or articles from blogs and sites you subscribed to, and your friends could comment on them. We know this sounds a lot like Facebook or Instagram or whatever, but trust us, it was way better because it wasn't popular or public enough to draw trolls or self-promoters. In the comments, we bantered about politics, shared recipes, and critiqued fashion bloggers' looks. Suddenly we weren't just hearing stories *about* each other's far-flung friends. We had elaborate inside jokes with them.

Five years after our karaoke night, the world would get a new vocabulary word for the kind of friend network that made it possible. #SquadGoals, an aspirational concept for how you'd like your crew of friends to be perceived, came into popular use courtesy of Taylor Swift, who famously began curating her set of model, actor, and musician friends in a stream of artfully arranged group photos on Instagram. She would later bring her squad members, all of whom happened to be hot, on stage during her sold-out world tour.

Swift wasn't the first or the only person to increase her power by highlighting her friend group. Rappers were shouting out their squads on hit songs long before it first appeared as a hashtagged goal in a white girl's Instagram caption. And centuries before that, squads were a military thing: a small, organized group or tactical unit going into battle together. As #SquadGoals became white-washed and feminized, though, it entered the popular conversation as a shorthand for a group of female friends so uncomplicated and cute it was aspirational. It also helped make marketable the idea that it is important to surround yourself with other women. Capitalism at work.

Gone are the days when women would casually say, "Oh, I don't have female friends." And gone, too, is the idea that every group of women is a toxic clique. Banding together is now seen as an essential survival tactic. All good things. But it's also a convenient and very low-lift public-relations exercise for any celebrity now, an easy way to seem likable and approachable.

Squads were an extension of a trope that has become familiar on TV shows about friendship. A fixed group that can fit on a single sofa in a coffee shop or around a four-top table at brunch makes for easy plotlines. And coincidentally, the number of people who can fit into a #SquadGoals image is about the same number who can be introduced in a pilot episode. The constraints of pop-culture plotlines support the idea that friend groups are fixed and exclusive, with specific traits assigned to different friends. ("I'm a Miranda.")

Another reason many people responded so well to the squad concept is because of how easy it is to perform friendship—not just for a celebrity like Swift, but for each of us, in front of our own social-media audience. Instagram feeds have become a way of showcasing how deep you roll. So it's easy to see how, as the squad concept got popular, it quickly soured. Even though squads were framed as feminist empowerment, they soon seemed like just another way for *Mean Girls*–style queen bees to show off their friendships in an exclusive way. *See? Look at our perfect group that you'll never be able to join and can only hope to replicate.* It was Shine Theory gone wrong.

Within a few years, even Swift was critical of squads. In an essay for *Elle*, she wrote that "never being popular as a kid was always an insecurity for me. . . . In my 20s I found myself surrounded by girls who wanted to be my friend. So I shouted it from the rooftops, posted pictures, and celebrated my newfound acceptance into a sisterhood, without realizing that other people might still feel the way I did when I felt so alone."

We don't have a squad. We have an ever-changing, interconnected web of friends. It's not something that's easily captured in a photo, but the friendweb is a helpful visual representation of the complex ways that the people we love connect and relate to each other. It encompasses our friends from childhood, college, places we've worked, various cities we've lived in, and social groups we've moved through. "When you marry someone, you marry their family" is a piece of pre-wedding advice that people have been doling out for generations. But it's also true that when you become close friends with someone, their friends become closer to you—and vice versa. There's only one way to be in a squad (and there are spots for only a few people), but there are a lot of different ways to be connected in a web.

Even the biggest friendships need other outlets: a lone friend cannot be your everything. The friendweb is an acknowledgment that we are all connected and that it takes a village to be a healthy, happy, successful person in the world. Like a spiderweb, a friendweb can be quite delicate or exceptionally strong. Some black widows' webs are so elastic that you can pluck the threads like guitar strings without breaking them, even as they stretch across vast distances. They're sort of like the far-flung but stable group of friends you've known forever and can reconnect with easily after time apart. Some spider silk outperforms Kevlar by 300 percent in its ability to absorb energy before breaking! Amazing, right? Our nearest and dearest core friendships, the ones that can withstand the biggest life challenges, are woven as if by this mega-resilient silk. Other spiderwebs are spun hastily and are thin enough to be blown away by a light breeze—like the friendships of circumstance you make at summer camp, or brand-new ones that have yet to be tested. So it is with a friendweb: depending on who's weaving, and under what circumstances, it can be unbreakably strong or whisper-thin. Every single one is different.

This is actually how academics who study friendship talk about interconnected humans too: as a web that is defined by the people in it. "Each individual is considered a node in a larger network," writes journalist Lydia Denworth in her book *Friendship*. And just because two people are connected does not mean they view their connection the same way. Denworth explains that what appears to be the very first map of social networks was drawn in 1938, when researchers recorded the friendships in a small town in Vermont. At its center was a woman dubbed "lady bountiful" who had been identified as the best friend of 17 people, despite her own claim that she had only two best friends. That's only a hint of how complex friendwebs can get. No two look alike. Lady bountiful thought her web had just three best friends in it. The other people in town would have drawn their webs quite differently.

Because the two of us have been close friends for so long, our webs intersect in a lot of important places. We're bound to each other not just directly but by a strong set of mutual friends. We've heard some people say that introducing their friends makes them anxious or that it's generally a bad idea, but we're of the persuasion that life is infinitely richer when friend circles converge. Fewer things make us happier than connecting our friends to each other. We both get a thrill from setting two people up on a friend date and then watching them create their own bond. It just feels right to have the different players in our lives know and cherish each other as well.

When we're at our best in the friendweb, we celebrate one another's successes and try to model healthy, accountable relationships. We try to treat each other's closest friends like in-laws: getting to know them, never bad-mouthing them, and staying in the loop about the big things that are going on in their lives. There is something very freeing about looking at the other people in our lives as models of accountability, happiness, and success rather than people we should be tracking in a competitive way. Friendwebs allow Shine Theory to flourish.

It's impossible to capture an entire friendweb with a camera. But when a lot of your friendships play out in digital spaces, technology can help you see your many connections. In 2013, the Massachusetts Institute of Technology's Media Lab created a tool that takes a person's Gmail data and uses it to generate a visual map of their social web. The tool, called Immersion, illustrates how you know everyone you've ever emailed with—which is to say, pretty much everyone in your life. It can tell you, with remarkable accuracy, exactly who introduced you to each new friend based on when they first popped up in your inbox. It can tell you which of your friends know each other too.

The Friendweb

The resulting web diagram provides the kind of satisfaction that conspiracy theorists must feel when they connect the dots. Anyone you've emailed with more than three times shows up as a "collaborator." On the visual map, each collaborator appears as a circle, with lines connecting them to others. The more you've emailed with someone, the bigger their circle is. You can slide a timeline at the bottom to see different people's circles grow and shrink. Exes disappear. Clusters of new coworkers pop up. You can actually watch friendships grow in importance, eclipsing other relationships.

When we used the tool, we both showed up as the biggest sun in the center of each other's inbox universe. Because we'd introduced each other to our friends from work and college and other places we'd lived, a lot of the same names popped up on our respective diagrams. Here were our friendwebs, laid out for us to see.

You may have heard of Dunbar's number, which says the average person's social network maxes out at 150 emotional connections. It comes from a theory by Robin Dunbar, a British anthropologist and evolutionary psychologist, who says that because humans evolved in small groups, we have a limited capacity for maintaining meaningful connections. Dunbar has found that most people have five people who are extremely close to them (aka Big Friendships and other intimate relationships), about 15 who are in regular contact with them and emotionally crucial, about 50 who are strongly and emotionally connected to them, and 80 who are slightly less connected but still a strong and important presence in their lives. These numbers are often represented in a diagram as a series of concentric circles, with an individual at the center and 150 people total across all the rings — the supposed maximum number of strong relationships that any one human can maintain.

For us, however, describing our friend network, even at a single moment in time, isn't as easy as drawing concentric circles. Some people are important by connection, even if we're not directly friends with them. Others are extremely important within a specific friend group or context, a corner of our web, but aren't the first person we call when we get some bad news. Others are historically and deeply important to us, but not the people we're texting every day. The friendweb is more complicated and more elaborately strung than a squad or Dunbar's concentric circles — and that's what makes it feel true to us.

William K. Rawlins, a pioneering scholar of friendship studies, told us that there is little to no research concerning dynamics within friend groups. Most of the academic work around friendship is focused on one-on-one relationships, as if they exist in a social vacuum. Culturally, there are no default rules for dealing with extensive and overlapping friend groups. Few people actually talk through their expectations and insecurities before the inevitable problems present themselves: What *do* you do when two people you've introduced to each other have a disagreement? What level of responsibility do you bear for a friend's behavior? When is it important to share information about what's happening with your other friendships, and when is it destructive gossip?

We learned the hard way that we have very different approaches to the mechanics of introducing, integrating, and maintaining the friends in our respective webs. Aminatou often connects her friends to each other for professional and personal

reasons. If she's hosting a party, she always makes sure to intro-
duce people who have things in common, and she smooths the
landing for anyone coming into a group where they know only
a few people. It's how she was raised. Ann almost never encoun-
tered strangers when she was growing up, as her family mingled
with the same crew of Catholic friends again and again (to such
a degree that she once referred to them as "the Church Cult").
As an adult she quickly embraced being a connector, but with
a laissez-faire attitude about friend intros. Ann doesn't feel the
need to assume responsibility for everything that might happen
between two people who meet through her. She figures that
they're both adults, and they can take things from there. In Aminatou's estimation, if you become the connector between two
close friends, sometimes you *do* have to get involved if one party
acts shitty toward the other. And, Aminatou believes, if you are
especially close with both of them and their disagreement is affecting a larger group dynamic, you might have a duty to mediate
or help clear the air.

If you experience the joy of having a vast, interconnected
friendweb, it's pretty much guaranteed you will go through the
pain of it too. We certainly have.

A few months before Ann's 30th birthday, she tried to think
of the ideal way to ring in a fresh decade. She had recently moved to Los Angeles for that dream editing job. She
had made a few friends there, but her job was so intense that
she was spending most of her time with her coworkers—and she
was dying for a break from the office. She also owed every single

friend a catch-up phone call and was craving time with long-distance members of her friendweb.

It was a time in both of our lives when we were traveling a lot for friends' bachelorette parties and weddings, and we were, quite frankly, over it. What if there was a trip designed only around comfort and relaxation—not impending nuptials—where we could do nothing for several days? The nearby Joshua Tree desert was perfect: convenient to Los Angeles but also an appealing January destination for friends who lived in wintry climates.

There is nothing that Aminatou loves more than a getaway to a warm location, and so when Ann floated the idea of renting a house in the desert, it was a no-brainer. Her caftans weren't going to wear themselves in DC.

The original email subject line was "desert lady birthday hangtimes," and in it, Ann invited women from all corners of her friendweb—women she'd met in high school, college, and her stints in San Francisco, DC, and Austin—to join her in Joshua Tree for her birthday. "I have decided that nothing would make me happier than to celebrate by hanging out in a house in southern California with every single woman I love and eating delicious food and watching bad movies and lounging in the hot tub and smoking so much weed and drinking so much whiskey and listening to so many jamz and generally basking in the greatness of it all," she wrote. "No pants. Only caftans." (This all still sounds great to us, except for the whole "spelling 'jamz' with a *z*" thing.) The responses were instantaneous and joyous. Aminatou made several spreadsheets to help with logistics. Everyone booked plane tickets to LAX and Palm Springs, and packed their flowiest garments.

Just like that, Desert Ladies, the purported low-drama, pants-less, braless, women-only vacation of our dreams, was born.

And it was glorious! We took up temporary residence in the gorgeous high desert with more than a dozen of our favorite women. There are many appealing things about an all-women getaway, but core to the Desert Ladies experience is a total escape from the male gaze. It is an explicitly non-romantic space, meaning that hookups between the women who attend are strongly discouraged and no romantic partners are invited. A platonic relaxation ideal. At Desert Ladies, the most important rule is what Aminatou's friends Brittany and Bethany dubbed Body's Choice: a simple philosophy that you should just let your body be your guide. It's an idea that can be surprisingly hard to follow in everyday life, when we're under pressure at work and subject to judgment whenever we opt for comfort rather than beauty or productivity.

In the desert, Body's Choice became a mantra. Should I sunbathe topless or make an elaborate snack? Body's Choice! Should I get stoned and swim, or get stoned and go hiking? Body's Choice! That first year, all 17 of us reveled in the fact that no one was commenting on our bodies *or* our choices. We noticed that dirty cups and plates seemed to be magically cleared away because we were all doing our part. There were nachos and cocktails, spontaneous dance breaks and face masks, and many meandering conversations. At midnight we bared our breasts to the moon and howled.

We didn't plan to make it a recurring event. But before the weekend was even over, there was already talk of how we had to do it again next year. We didn't pause to think about what might be difficult, weird, or cliquish about attempting to re-create this event annually. It did not occur to us that a friendweb is not only too big to fit inside an Instagram-cropped frame but also too big to fit inside a single house. We knew we wanted to repeat this trip.

The next year, Ann sent another group email, this time with the subject line "Pantsless Ladies of the Desert II: Return to Joshua Tree." That second year was bigger and bolder. The original 17 women were invited, but by this point Ann's LA friendweb had expanded to include a half dozen others. Several of them came with a plus-one, so the final tally ended up being 26. Ann found a weird house with a ton of bunk beds in Palm Desert that was clearly owned by a religious family. The owners had painted the names of books of the Bible above each of the bedroom doors. Someone started jokingly referring to all of us as "sisterwives." The caftans, edibles, and moon howling were in full effect once again. Aminatou met some of Ann's core LA friends for the first time in person (they'd already exchanged dozens of messages online), and there were endless "I feel like I already know yous" exchanged.

After that second year, Ann felt like all of these first-time meetings and plus-one guests were the perfect way to carry Desert Ladies forward as a tradition. Sure, it originally began with her birthday and she was the person who took the initiative to send the emails and book the venue, but she no longer felt like it was "her" weekend. She was also scared to take full responsibility for Desert Ladies as an invitation-only space. She believed that after she invited someone once, they were grandmothered in to all future trips. Desert Ladies, in her mind, was now a communal experience that was shaped by the women who attended it. And so the group grew in a way that wasn't just tied to Ann's personal friendweb. All told, 50 women signed up to attend the third year. We were going to need a bigger space.

What we found was Areolas, a run-down "clothing optional" resort in Desert Hot Springs that offered a dirt-cheap price for us to rent it out entirely for a week. (A masseuse once remarked to us that she had never seen so many people with clothes on in the confines of the compound.) It had a hot tub in which 30 people could sit comfortably (we swam lazy laps in it), a large goddess statue, and one square of poolside concrete that had been marked by boob-prints in the wet cement. We'd found a new home.

What we didn't realize was how stretched we would feel by the scale and scope of hosting 50 women. This is more people than are invited to some weddings, which was, shockingly, neither a deterrent nor a red flag. Nor was the fact that Ann was traveling out of the country for much of the year leading up to the third Desert Ladies, and she couldn't actually handle several of the details. Ann appointed a logistics council to help her figure out how to plan meals and share expenses.

Aminatou stepped up and organized a taco truck for Saturday night. She was also tasked with wrangling finances. Up to this point, Ann would put the whole trip on her credit card and would be reimbursed, but that was not possible for a party of 50—which meant a lot of reminders to get people to download payment apps and follow instructions. The fact that we were both at the center of figuring out these logistics contributed to the impression throughout our friendweb that we spoke for each other. When Ann was in a different time zone or not responding to an email, people reached out to Aminatou to ask questions or for help because, naturally, it seemed that she would know. Indeed,

Aminatou sometimes thought of Desert Ladies as "our trip," meaning her and Ann.

A side effect of the group growing so big was that the connections between all these people in the friendweb grew more difficult to understand. Which people were best friends of many years, and which were effectively strangers? It wasn't clear. There was a noticeably bigger contingent of LA-based women that year, and Aminatou assumed they were all close friends of Ann's. If she had actually asked Ann about her relationship with these people, she would have found out that some of them were new friends and others were just plus-ones. This should have been one of the first indications that the sprawling web was about to get tangled. A good rule of thumb is that you should be able to keep track of how everyone in the web is connected and their level of intimacy. As the group expanded, the ties between different people at Desert Ladies became less apparent. And to complicate matters, the group had grown big enough that a few of the women who were invited had developed some degree of tension between them.

This illustrated an important lesson we were just beginning to learn about our friendweb: as it becomes larger and more interconnected, everything from innocent miscommunications to whispered rumors can potentially rupture it. Unspoken, unaddressed problems can tear the most strongly woven friendwebs apart. We know now that it's better to acknowledge that problems are inevitable in a group, and straightforwardly discuss them—ideally, in a spirit of generosity—so that they don't fester.

As the third Desert Ladies trip approached, Aminatou called Ann to discuss something that was upsetting her. Aminatou isn't interested in rehashing the details of what happened, but the gist of it was, she was betrayed by a woman who was now part of the Desert Ladies crew. It seemed like the woman might be attending the upcoming trip, and Aminatou wanted to talk it through. She wanted to figure out her own next steps and decide if she felt comfortable being there. She wanted to vent.

Ann listened to Aminatou's story about the incident and agreed that the woman had behaved badly. But Ann interpreted Aminatou's venting as a tacit request for intervention—even though it hadn't occurred to Aminatou that the woman could be disinvited, and she wasn't asking that of Ann. Aminatou was not the first Desert Lady to approach Ann that year to make a pointed inquiry about whether another woman would be in attendance. Ann was trying to navigate the fact that two other people on the invite list had fallen out over a work issue.

There were other preoccupations. As the trip grew closer, women were dropping out, asking if their friends could join, or wondering if they could just stop by for a day. The attendance list and transportation details seemed to shift daily. Ann couldn't admit it, but she was feeling overwhelmed by this role she had created for herself. She had considered only the upsides of connecting every corner of her friendweb at an annual event. Prior to this conflict, it hadn't occurred to Ann that inviting her entire social circle into a single space might force her to make difficult decisions if disagreements arose. Even though she was so much closer to Aminatou than to the woman who had hurt her, and *of course* she would rather have Aminatou in attendance, Ann did not want to be some sort of caftan-clad Judge Judy, not only deciding who was wrong and who was right but also expected to mete out punishment in the form of a revoked invitation to this desert trip. Ann could tell that these unresolved feelings about her responsibilities for this trip were a problem, but she pushed them aside in order to keep planning.

Aminatou, who had no idea that Ann was dealing with other disagreements within the friendweb, was taken aback by what she perceived as Ann's complete lack of concern. The incident made her start to doubt that Ann was loyal to her in the same ways she was loyal to Ann.

If you're thinking this sounds like a lot of drama for two "low-drama mamas," we agree. People hurt and misunderstand each other all the time—it's inevitable, even between two people who know each other very well. We can see now that "low-drama" was a cover for our tendency to avoid conflict, a way we both tried to minimize problems that actually needed to be addressed. And ignoring what was happening didn't make those problems disappear. It made them worse.

In a series of side conversations, Ann told the women who were invited—Aminatou included—that they should handle their problems with each other directly and that they could each decide whether or not they wanted to attend.

The decision would forever affect how Aminatou felt about Desert Ladies. All Aminatou heard in that instance was that she was a burden to Ann. She also felt underappreciated and dismissed and that the labor she had done over the past two years to make the trip possible seemed to have been largely invisible.

It would be years before we could talk directly about what happened at the third Desert Ladies. Ann has continued to convene the trip, albeit in a scaled-down way. Aminatou has made the occasional appearance but hasn't really been back in years. At first people had a lot of questions about Aminatou's absence, but Ann told them it was simply a scheduling issue.

Our blind spots are now so obvious: We love to have a good time, so gathering a group of our favorite women made sense. But we never discussed anything deeper than logistics because we assumed that we were on the same page when it came to the friendweb. Oh boy, were we not on the same page. We weren't even reading the same book.

Today we have to wonder, how much grief would we have saved ourselves if we had just talked about it more openly? Aminatou really wishes she would have said, "Hey, Ann! This really blows. I don't actually care if this person comes on the trip or not, but I need you to acknowledge that this is fucked-up and that I feel tender about it." And Ann wishes she had told Aminatou, "I am feeling extremely stressed and unsure about something that's supposed to be *fun*. I care so much about you feeling welcome and happy at this event. If her presence will ruin your enjoyment of the weekend, I will disinvite her."

But we didn't do any of that.

It might seem like this is a petty little story about a group vacation gone awry, but the feelings involved were not petty. It was the first tremor that indicated there might be a fault line in our friendship. Aminatou felt that tremor but didn't say anything to Ann.

Ann didn't feel it at all.

SEVEN

••

The Trapdoor

It was one of those perfect California nights, not too cold or too hot. Ann's backyard was strung with lights and punctuated with the cheerful buzz of conversation as people milled around with glasses of rosé in hand. She had offered up her patio as the venue for a friend's birthday party. And—even better—Aminatou happened to be in town. She was in Los Angeles for a work trip and had been looking forward to attending the backyard soiree because she knew and liked the birthday girl and many of the other guests.

When she showed up, the party was already in full swing. Aminatou found that the snacks were delicious and the mood lovely. But what should have been a fun night celebrating and catching up with friends turned sour when Aminatou noticed that she was the only Black person milling around Ann's back patio.

Aminatou was thrown off guard. It felt surreal to be at a gathering like this. She knew Ann didn't only have white friends, yet here Aminatou was, scanning the yard for the slightest hint of melanin. Nothing. Not even a racially ambiguous tan.

Could this really be possible? After all these years of knowing Ann? Why was Aminatou the only Black person at this party? She was screaming inside: *Where are your Black friends?*

Surely the other guests could sense her panic. She felt a sinking sensation, like she was falling through the brick tiles of Ann's patio.

The writer Wesley Morris calls this experience the trapdoor of racism. "For people of color, some aspect of friendship with white people involves an awareness that you could be dropped through a trapdoor of racism at any moment, by a slip of the tongue, or at a campus party, or in a legislative campaign," he wrote in 2015. "But it's not always anticipated." The trapdoor describes the limited level of comfort that Black people can feel around white people who are part of their lives in a meaningful way. Even if these white people decide they will confront racism every day, it's guaranteed they will sometimes screw up and disappoint the Black people they know.

Race plays out differently in every friendship. And not all interracial relationships involve a Black person and a white person, but ours does. So that's what we're going to talk about here.

Contrary to what pop culture would have us believe (looking at you, *Green Book*), most interracial friendships aren't actually rooted in deep conversations around racial difference. Not in the beginning, at least. Like all relationships, interracial friendships begin when two people bond over the things they have in common. (Remember our story of sameness?) In a conversation with us, Morris pointed out that in some interracial friendships, there are things both people instinctively know not to speak about. "There's a comfort that you have in these relationships that is somewhat contingent upon not going there. Everybody has a boundary, a place where the relationship just kind of tacitly knows not to go," he says. "But there will be some incident, and normally it is a thing that is beyond both parties' control, that forces you to go there."

"Some incident." Sigh. Aminatou and many of her Black friends know to dread this incident. The incident doesn't necessarily even have to be caused by the white friend. Morris says it can involve "the white friend's friends, or the white friend's family, or a circumstance in which you're experiencing racism or general unpleasantness that tips into racism, and the white friend is kind of like, 'Uh, I think you, nonwhite friend, are overreacting to whatever is happening right now.'" In a split second, Morris says, the trapdoor opens. The Black friend is forced to reevaluate the friendship based on an incident that can, on the surface, seem relatively innocent.

This is different from the way Aminatou feels when she experiences more overt forms of racism, like the time a biker called her a nigger in an Oklahoma gas station shortly after she moved to the United States. She's always on high alert for things strangers might say to her, but her guard is down when she's with people she knows. With strangers, it feels like bracing for impact while her plane crashes, but when it's an incident with someone she loves, like a white friend or intimate partner, it doesn't feel as dramatic. Morris says that in these cases, it's more like a drop of mustard falling on your pants. You notice and you feel uncomfortable about it, but the person who dropped the mustard does not even register what has happened. Now you have to decide whether to say something and call attention to the stain. Either way, there is awkwardness and discomfort. And pain never lurks too far behind racial discomfort.

The birthday party was exactly like that. Aminatou left early that night and didn't bring it up with Ann immediately. *This is the kind of thing you file away as a data point, a discrete unit of information*, she thought to herself. Every Black person who intimately knows a white person has their own data set. One data point doesn't tell the full story, but if you gather enough context, you can start making sense of the whole picture.

Aminatou waited to talk about it because she needed to sort out her feelings. It wasn't the first time she had been the only Black person in a room. It happened at work all the time, actually. It even happened at many smaller parties Ann had hosted over the years. (Listen, all of your brunches cannot look like a college-recruitment brochure.) But this felt different. After years of living far apart, Aminatou wasn't present at every gathering Ann hosted in LA, so it was jarring to drop in on one that looked like this. *Do I even know you?* she wondered. If this was how Ann's life was organized now, Aminatou wasn't sure of her place in it. She also wondered what other signs she had missed over the years.

Another reason Aminatou didn't bring it up right away is that, on its face, the incident itself seemed a little silly. It was just a birthday party! Someone else's birthday party, at that. *Why was this such a big deal?* But she knew it was not a small deal because of the feelings that came bubbling up to the surface for her. She felt uncomfortable, and she was struggling with the fact that she felt she couldn't talk to Ann about it just yet.

Aminatou believed that if one of their friends had come to her and Ann about a similar situation, Ann would have risen to the occasion. Ann would have asked the white person to take a long, critical look at the decisions that led them to have no Black friends present at such a large gathering. But it's always easier to dole out advice for someone else's problems. And when it comes to race, it's even easier for well-meaning white people to call out someone else's behavior while ignoring their own. They do it all the time.

We had discussed plenty of times how disgraceful it was for people to plan or participate in all-white panels at professional conferences. (All-male panels? Also not great!) A birthday party isn't a professional event, but the point still stands. If you're a white person and your weekend trips, baby showers, and dinner parties are all-white affairs, this signals a few things to your Black friends. At best it shows that your gatherings are places where only white people are welcome. At worst it leads them to assume that they're your only Black friend, a token you collected like a diversity Pokémon. Not actually a real friend. For white people, being in all-white spaces is a choice they make, not something that accidentally happens when they don't double-check the guest list.

Aminatou was disappointed when Ann didn't bring up the party incident first. Ann's silence had made Aminatou doubt herself about whether or not the incident was a big deal. Aminatou felt that without making excuses, Ann should have acknowledged how messed up it was. Aminatou knew it wasn't Ann's party and she hadn't made the guest list, but *Aminatou* shouldn't be the only one paying attention to race. Liberal white people like Ann often say they aren't afraid to talk about racial difference, but Morris points out that "if you're a Black person in America, odds are if you're going to have an intimate relationship with a white person the subject of race is going to come up because you're introducing it."

This was about so much more than a single unfortunate birthday party. It highlighted an unbridgeable gap between the two of us.

This isn't exactly the plot of *Get Out* (even though the Sunken Place is very real), but Ann is a white person living within a culture that has some extremely deeply ingrained and fucked-up ideas about race. Which is to say that racism is structural. There is a complex system by which racism is developed, maintained, and protected. It's not just a term that applies to those who personally hate people of other races. It's baked into our political system, our art and culture, our financial structures, our ideas about value and communication. Which means that it affects everyone, no matter what their personal views on race happen to be. No matter what their closest friends look like. It's in everyday experiences and fleeting moments. It's everywhere.

This is what makes race a different kind of challenge than the stretches we experienced when Aminatou got sick or when Ann moved far away. Those challenges live within the scope of our friendship. Race is bigger than our friendship. We, and all of our dynamics, live within *it*. And so we can't reduce our difficulties in navigating racial difference to a single before-and-after "teachable moment." In the grand scheme of our friendship, the birthday party wasn't a huge incident. It's just one of many small ways that racism creeps into our relationship. And one of many that were difficult for us to talk about in real time.

We share many of the same high-level ideas about race and the way it contributes to inequalities and injustices in our world. We are adept at talking about the way racism plays out in the news or culture. We feel comfortable discussing the racism Aminatou has experienced at work or out in the world, and racist incidents Ann has observed with other friends.

But when Ann becomes the source of the pain that Aminatou is feeling? We have a much harder time talking about that.

For as long as she can remember, Aminatou was acutely aware of the racial divide between Black and white people. Her earliest racist memory is of a girl in the first grade who refused to stand next to her during the class photo. She claimed Aminatou was "too dark and ugly." (Too bad, little French girl! People love to ask Aminatou for selfies now.) But Aminatou also lived in West Africa, where almost everyone looked like her. She wasn't a minority, and diversity was something she thought of in terms of nationality. Even though it was glossed over in French school, Aminatou's mother made sure she had a robust African history education. She learned the stories of Aminatou, the great Hausa warrior queen, and Samory Touré, the hero who led the resistance against French colonial forces in present-day Guinea. She heard the stories of the ancestor her father is named after, Alpha Yaya of Labé, who refused to cede the province he was in charge of to the French and died for it. Aminatou knew about the kingdoms, the art, the science, and the innovations of the people who looked like her. The little French girl had hurt her feelings, but Aminatou never believed for a second that there was any truth to her ignorant words.

Understanding racial dynamics in college proved trickier to navigate. In her earliest days in the United States, Aminatou would characterize every uncomfortable experience as a broad cultural misunderstanding with Americans in general. It took her a while to realize that race was actually at the center of so much of the discomfort she felt: white people touching her hair, repeated comments about how "articulate" she was, the "hey girl" finger waving and neck rolling that white gay men were so comfortable doing around her. She was told repeatedly that she was "not like other Black people," which caused her great distress.

When Aminatou finally opened up to other Black international students about this, she was relieved that she wasn't imagining it. These conversations illuminated that they were having the same experiences too and that it was blackness, not foreign-ness, that was at the root of it all. The relief gave way to consternation at American race relations. (If you're from a different country and agreeing, don't worry, your country has messed-up race relations too. Yes, even you, Canada.) She also grappled with the fact that, despite being on the receiving end of anti-Black racism, she had enough cultural dexterity to navigate a lot of white environments in a way that some of her African-American friends could not. White Americans seemed much more comfortable with a boarding-school-educated foreigner. And because of that, she felt an added responsibility to never let racism slide or she would be complicit in it too.

Aminatou has no fear of calling out bigoted Twitter trolls or taking on strangers who use a racial slur. Where she's been disarmed is closer to home: the college friend's parents who never stop marveling at how "good" her English is, the friend who often confuses her Asian colleagues for one another, the boyfriend whose grandmother insisted on calling her "Tina Turner" (Aminatou still gets a full-body cringe when she thinks of that one). The closer the relationship, the more awkward and sensitive it is to address the offense. Some people will act as if these incidents are just misdemeanors easily waved off, but Aminatou firmly believes that interracial intimacy is the only context in which "broken windows" theory is actually relevant: any visible signs of crime encourage further crime! You have to call it out or it will erode your relationship.

If racism exists on a scale—from the 1 or 2 of someone calling her another Black person's name ("hello, Dayo!") to the full-blown 10 of Trump-style white nationalism—then for a time, Aminatou believed that dealing with a little bit of it (a 1 here, a 2 there) was the price you paid for having white folks in your life. But the older she got, the less flexible she became about this. A lot of her white friends were grandmothered in under a more lax regime. More often than not, she was their first and sometimes only Black friend. Today it would be impossible for her to befriend anyone who didn't already have significant relationships with Black people.

Aminatou is not the only person who applies this standard when she considers whether to befriend a white person. We talked to another interracial friend pair, Saeed and Isaac, who have been in a Big Friendship for almost a decade. Saeed was initially wary of becoming friends with Isaac, who pursued him at a writing conference. "There are just so many friendly-looking, smiling, flannel-wearing white guys in publishing. You know what I mean?" Saeed says. "I remember having that hesitation of 'I don't even want to give this stranger an opportunity to disappoint me.'" When Saeed finally let Isaac in, "he just kept proving himself in unexpected ways, you know?" Isaac had been homeless for part of his childhood, and by talking about not just race but also class, they were able to forge a path forward. Saeed explains, "For whatever reason, I think we were perfectly calibrated." It was also noteworthy to Saeed that Isaac grew up in a predominantly Black neighborhood and has Black family members. Saeed wasn't Isaac's only significant relationship with a Black person.

Aminatou had some similar assurances about Ann. We were introduced to each other by a Black woman, after all. Dayo and Aminatou did the thing where, without saying too many words, Black people assess their white homies. Dayo indicated that Ann was a white woman who wouldn't go out of her way to embarrass herself or either of them.

Aminatou expected that Ann would know how to pronounce her name correctly, that she would not ask basic questions about her hair or use the N word while singing along to the radio. If Aminatou pointed out that something she experienced was racist, she knew that Ann wouldn't play devil's advocate. That instead of tiptoeing around the issue, Ann would understand why it hurts when people refuse to talk about race, and that even when we weren't together, Ann would never let a racist comment slide. That Ann would try her damn best to step outside of her privilege and into Aminatou's shoes to see the world from her perspective, where race permeates everything. Isaac told us that he works to be someone Saeed can be proud of, and that's exactly how Ann feels about her friendship with Aminatou. She tries to live up to Aminatou's expectations.

This also explains why, as Aminatou wandered around the backyard party, she felt that the scene reflected poorly not just on Ann but on *her*. Aminatou knew that, fairly or unfairly, some people trusted Ann's racial politics because of Aminatou's relationship with her. She didn't want to be Ann's racial endorser, but that's often a side effect of interracial friendship. Ann committing a low-level racial "oops" wasn't just a momentary disappointment to Aminatou; it had larger ramifications. And, worst of all, Ann didn't seem to be aware of this.

A minatou finally brought up the birthday party several months later, when she was with Ann in person and having dinner at the bar of a nice restaurant. Aminatou described what it was like for her to walk into Ann's backyard and see all those white guests. "I just didn't think that would ever happen at your house or an event you planned," she said. "It was disorienting and makes me feel like I am no longer welcome in your home. I also resent that I have to be the one to bring it up, because my hope is that you also noticed."

Ann felt defensive. "I hear you, but it wasn't my party," she said. "I didn't make the guest list." Ann had noticed that Aminatou left early that night. But, Ann said, "I thought you were just tired from traveling." She took a breath and a sip of her cocktail and continued, "I did notice how white the party was, but I didn't take responsibility for that fact." She took a few more breaths. "I really regret that. I'm really sorry that I didn't bring it up first.

And I'm even more sorry that this made you feel unwelcome in my house. You are always welcome in my house." Ann felt horrible that a situation in her own home had made one of her closest friends feel so alienated. She had let Aminatou down.

We kept talking and trying to express what this was bringing up for each of us, but there was no neat resolution. It was finally all on the table—or, at least, we weren't actively holding anything back—but that wasn't a relief at all. We sat side by side, searching each other's faces for signs of understanding. Near the end of our conversation, the bartender sent us two free shots. "I don't know what you two are talking about," she said, "but you look like you need this."

It's telling that Ann's first feeling in the conversation was defensiveness. It flared up so quickly—faster, even, than feelings of sorrow or even regret. Like a lot of white people, Ann was raised on a steady diet of "race doesn't matter" and "treat everyone with equal respect." Which sounds great and is preferable to overtly racist messaging but is not a particularly meaningful thing to hear if you're raised in an extremely segregated environment. Her hometown was about 98 percent white, and growing up, everyone Ann knew was Catholic, with German and Irish ancestors and a pair of hetero parents. Ann absorbed a lot of high-level messages about how difference is cool, but most of the characters in the books she read were white. Somewhere in her parents' basement there is a VHS tape of local TV news footage featuring Ann representing Jamaica at her school's multicultural fair. But it's obvious that learning the lyrics to "Day-O" was useless training for how to have interracial relationships in a world rife with racism and inequality.

Ann made her first nonwhite friends when she went away to

college. During her freshman year, the campus Amnesty International group was doing an anti-death-penalty action that focused on the racial disparities on death row. Ann and another white member of the group came up with what they thought was an eye-opening message that would really get their fellow students' attention: they would frame this problem as modern-day lynching. Rhetorically they thought it made sense. After all, 42 percent of death sentences are handed to Black Americans, who are just 13 percent of the overall population. But Ann and her friend, who was a white guy, had this idea—god, she can't believe she's even going to admit this—to hang nooses from trees around campus above placards with statistics about the death penalty. (If you are screaming at how horrible and misguided this idea is, know that Ann is screaming with you.)

The night before they were going to do this, their friend Daanish piped up to suggest, oh so gently, that *maybe* this action would be interpreted as incredibly threatening to Black students on campus. That *maybe* it would have the opposite of the intended effect. Ann would like to take this opportunity to say, "THANK YOU, DAANISH, for saving us from ourselves." They still put up the placards with the statistics, but discarded the noose idea. It was Ann's first experience with a friend of a different race doing emotional labor to save her from herself, though she wouldn't have described it that way at the time. She didn't have that vocabulary yet, and she was still burning with the shame of having made such a terrible suggestion in the first place. She was mortified that she hadn't even considered how this idea would have traumatized Black students.

Here's a harsh reality of friendship that crosses big divides in privilege and identity: stretching to account for these differences usually doesn't go both ways in equal measure. When it comes to interracial friendships that involve a white person, it's likely that the nonwhite friend is going to feel more negatively stretched, while the white friend gets to have a "learning experience." Sometimes this happens through the daily stuff of friendship: sharing frustrations and joys. Other times, though, it happens more explicitly, like when Ann's friend Daanish had to be like, "Um, you think you're an ally but actually you're going to traumatize people." (Again, thank you, Daanish.)

For white people like Ann, who have close friends of other races, it can be a delicate line between constructively learning about injustice through your friends' experiences and turning your friends into a personal racial-education service. As we've said, this is one stretch that cannot go both ways equally. There are things that Aminatou came to our friendship already understanding about Ann's existence because Aminatou is steeped in white culture, and things Ann will never fully understand about Aminatou's experience of the world. Aminatou has often been a foil for Ann to learn about difference.

Take, for example, what happened with Desert Ladies. At the time, we didn't talk about the conflict in terms of race. But later, Aminatou was able to articulate to Ann that a major pain point in that moment was that she had felt reduced to an Angry Black Woman. This hateful stereotype dates back to 19th-century minstrel shows, in which white men in blackface and fat suits appeared in skits mocking African-American women. The point was "to make them look less than human, unfeminine, ugly," Blair Kelley, associate professor of history at North Carolina

State University, told the BBC. "Their main way of interacting with the men around them was to scream and fight and come off angry, irrationally so, in response to the circumstances around them." This insidious trope is unfortunately still very liberally deployed. Just read coverage of Serena Williams and you'll get the picture.

Expressing anger comes at a cost for women like Aminatou. Being labeled as angry ensures that Black women are not allowed to experience a full range of emotions: vulnerability, fear, hurt, or fragility. Brittney Cooper, historian and author of *Eloquent Rage: A Black Feminist Discovers Her Superpower*, told NPR, "Whenever someone weaponizes anger against black women, it is designed to silence them. It is designed to discredit them and to say that they are overreacting, that they are being hypersensitive, that their reaction is outsized."

Ann was aware that Aminatou often felt she had to tread lightly to avoid being seen this way. But Ann also failed to see how Aminatou might also be treading lightly with *her*. It didn't occur to her that's what was happening during their discussion about who was and wasn't attending Desert Ladies. She didn't even consider that Aminatou might be holding back some emotion, that years of tiptoeing around a stereotype might limit how comfortable Aminatou felt in expressing to Ann that she was upset. Years later, when we finally had a frank conversation about how all of this played into the way Aminatou was feeling about Desert Ladies, things finally clicked into place for Ann. A white aha moment.

Aminatou let Ann know that throughout their friendship she has had to modulate her emotions as to never appear too annoyed or to be honest about something upsetting her. In her Desert

Ladies conflict aversion, Ann got to appear as cool as a cucumber, a magnanimous white woman, while Aminatou had to suppress her hurt feelings so as not to rock the boat. It is a dynamic that has replicated itself at various points in our relationship. Aminatou felt a huge burden lifted off her when she shared this particular data point with Ann. It is not Ann's fault that Aminatou is often reduced to racist stereotypes, but Aminatou wants Ann to acknowledge the work that comes with being friends with a white person. And to do more work herself: to not just recognize that racist stereotypes exist but account for them without Aminatou having to point out that they are present in our interactions.

Pat Parker's poem "For the White Person Who Wants to Know How to Be My Friend" begins with two pieces of advice: "The first thing you do is to forget that i'm Black. / Second, you must never forget that i'm Black." After building a story of sameness and years of feeling in sync about almost everything, Ann had grasped the first rule but neglected the second.

When we asked Dayo whether she ever felt burdened by being a friend's de facto racial-education service, she pointed out the tension between wanting your experience to be intrinsically, fully understood and having to educate your friends of different races. When it comes to intimate relationships, "I feel like you can't hold people fully accountable for things that you haven't communicated to them," she says. "So I spend a lot of time communicating my race politics when there isn't a live conflict. Which I think hopefully de-risks having the conversation when there is. While I hate the tax of being an integrator, I think education can be extremely casual." She says that the more time she spends around someone, the less necessary it becomes to translate her feelings into an explicit conversation. "My closest confidantes can tell you what is going to make me feel vulnerable or irritated or when I'm going to be like, 'Ugh, oh my god, white people.' It's knowable," she says, laughing. It's also, she acknowledges, a pain in the ass to have to think about this at all. "Sometimes you just want to watch YouTube."

Here are some of the "being a white friend" feelings Ann has had: Trying to summon up the courage to overcome her fear of saying the wrong thing. The shame of having to google basic things she feels she should know, like how much it costs for Black women to get braids or how to pronounce her South Asian friends' names. The sadness of realizing that her friends are actively choosing whether to make an issue of something that Ann hasn't even noticed. But Ann does not often voice these feelings out loud to her friends. It's not the feelings themselves that are a problem. It's what she does with the feelings that matters.

When Ann wrote the article explaining Shine Theory that fully credited Aminatou as the coauthor of the idea, you can guess what happened next: people solely attributed Shine Theory to Ann. This wasn't Ann's fault—people have been failing to credit Black women for their genius ideas since the dawn of time—but it could have easily caused strife between us. The reason it hasn't is that, without being asked, Ann began sending firm and extremely annoyed emails and tweets asking people to credit Aminatou when they cite Shine Theory. She still does this regularly. Aminatou appreciates that Ann doesn't just recognize the mistake; she acts to correct the record.

And then there are other times when Ann just doesn't get it. She fails to step up—like when she wasn't the first to bring up the overwhelming whiteness of the birthday party. This is when the trapdoor opens.

You don't get to pick your family of origin or the place you grow up. But you do get to choose your friends, and those choices say something about the kind of world you want for yourself. This is one of the many ways friendship is political. We're not just talking about whether you have people in your life who voted for the opposite party or whether you're carpooling to the protest march with your friends. We're talking about small-*p* politics, or "the total complex of relations between people living in society," as the dictionary puts it. White people can't be surprised that white supremacists are marching in the streets if their own lives are racially segregated. The choices that each of us makes every day about who we include in our lives end up shaping the larger world we live in.

There's no definitive way to determine how common interracial friendships are. Simply asking people if they have a friend of a different race is ineffective, given that people who are surveyed are likely to include mere acquaintances as friends in an effort to appear well-rounded and open-minded. "Both white and black Americans prove to be more optimistic than accurate in their descriptions of their personal race relations," writes the sociologist Kathleen Odell Korgen in her book *Crossing the Racial Divide: Close Friendships Between Black and White Americans*. She cites a survey from 1999, which found that 42 percent of white people said they had close friends of another race. Seems like a decently high number, right? But when those white people were asked to write down the names of their closest friends and *then* identify their races, only 6 percent of whites listed a Black friend. When the same questions were posed to Black people, 62 percent said they had a white friend, and 15 percent wrote down the name of a white person as one of their six closest.

A few researchers have found more creative ways to get around the self-reporting problem. In 2006, the demographer Brent Berry set out to discover how common interracial friendships really are by examining more than 1,000 photographs of wedding parties. Berry reasoned that people typically include their closest friends in their bridal parties, leaving little doubt that bridesmaids and groomsmen were truly close to the couple getting married.

To say that Berry's results were eye-opening would be an understatement. He found that just 3.7 percent of whites were close enough to Black people to include them in their wedding parties. Meanwhile, 22.2 percent of Black people had white groomsmen or bridesmaids.

It's worth pointing out that people of different races may have different motivations for self-segregating. Researchers have found that Black children segregate as a self-protective measure. "What we find is that in spaces where there is racial inequity, that is a protective response," Cinzia Pica-Smith, associate professor at Assumption College, told NPR. "White children, however, self-segregate because of prejudice against kids of different races." And white people are responsible for the institutional reasons the racial divide is so gaping in the first place. Black people aren't the ones who redlined neighborhoods and perpetuated hiring discrimination and decided they were super into school segregation. It's white people who have been disproportionately in power for centuries, or, more accurately, running a system designed to reward whiteness, that has ensured that race plays a role in where people live and work and go to school. All while continually voicing the idea that race shouldn't matter and everything is a meritocracy.

You can see this easy-way-out attitude toward interracial relationships play out in pop culture too. All too often, diverse families and friendships are presented simplistically—at worst as mere tokenism or at best as an aspirational ideal, with little or no depiction of the candor, self-examination, and often painful confrontation it takes for people of different races to understand and support one another. From the Black best friend stereotype in movies to wholesome images of interracial families in ads pushing everything from breakfast cereal to laundry detergent, it's as if, in a rush toward the mythical bliss of post-racial harmony, we (well, not we, but white people) have skipped over truth and jumped straight to reconciliation.

Saying over and over that race *shouldn't* matter distracts from the fact that it still does. Especially to people in intimate interracial relationships.

I n a 1975 lecture on race and politics, the writer Toni Morrison summed up the true function of racism: "It keeps you from doing your work. It keeps you explaining, over and over again, your reason for being. Somebody says you have no language and so you spend 20 years proving that you do. Somebody says your head isn't shaped properly so you have scientists working on the fact that it is. Somebody says that you have no art so you dredge that up. Somebody says that you have no kingdoms and so you dredge that up. None of that is necessary."

Racism is also exhausting and paranoia-inducing within a friendship. Aminatou knows it all too well: you wish and pray that your friend doesn't do or say anything racist but you know full well that they're capable of it anyway. If Big Friendship is built on trust, can it even exist if the trapdoor is always threatening to swing open?

For both of us, talking about race has been the only way to process its effect on our relationship and to make sense of the fact that racism is both personal and not personal at the same time. If friends don't discuss the racism that arises in their own friendship, it can ring hollow when the white friend tries to express dismay about, say, a white supremacist event that is all over the news. Why should a person of color trust that this white friend is truly invested in being the solution instead of the problem? In our friendships, we don't just say "don't be racist," we also say "racism exists and this is how we deal with it."

Race is not a challenge to overcome. It's something to be constantly aware of. As the great feminist Flo Kennedy once said, "Freedom is like taking a bath. You got to keep doing it every day." In other words, it's not just what you say or what you purport to believe. It's something you have to constantly reinforce with your actions. We don't share the birthday party story because it's a big dramatic, pivotal moment in our lives. We share it because it's the kind of thing we have had to contend with—and talk through.

There is a strong case for Aminatou's rule about never being anyone's starter Black friend. Researchers have found that interracial relationships tend to end sooner than same-race relationships if it's the *only* interracial relationship for one or both parties. In other words, being in an intimate relationship with someone of another race is a particular type of stretch, and you're likely to be better at it if you are doing it in more than one relationship. Unlike other stretches, it will never stop being a challenge. But you can improve. Get stronger.

The stretch of interracial friendship requires different skills from each person. In our case, Aminatou has to remain flexible about when to educate and communicate. Ann has to own that her silences around racial issues have meaning and she has to push past moments of discomfort to stay accountable. The sociologist Robin DiAngelo told us in an interview that this discomfort is also a "potential door" to better actions, and she challenges white people to meet their friends halfway by taking a risk. "What's the worst that's going to happen to you?" she asks. "Come on." She notes that the fear white people feel about addressing race is not remotely equivalent to the terror that Black people experience on a daily basis as a result of white inaction.

Often, the accountability question Ann asks herself is: Would I be able to look my Black friends in the eye and describe how I handled this situation? If the answer is not "absolutely yes"—and, in all honesty, the answer is not always "absolutely yes"—that's how Ann knows she has to do better.

We know that we are never going to stop having hard conversations about race. The best we can hope for is that there's always a sympathetic bartender in the vicinity.

EIGHT

..

See You on the Internet

We can't remember exactly when our friend Gina Delvac, a brilliant radio producer, first suggested we start a podcast. We do remember that we got serious about the idea in January 2014, when we decided the show should have a chatty, conversational format. We would just call each other and talk about the news and culture headlines, and we'd name the podcast *Call Your Girlfriend*, after the Robyn song we'd spent so many late nights dancing to. We bought the URL, which is our way of really committing to a project, and we emailed our favorite audio producer. "Yessssss," Gina replied, and quoted a line from the song: "it's time we had the talk."

Gina's excitement was critical, because she had all the expertise. She curated podcast playlists for us, so we could familiarize ourselves with the medium. She told us which microphones to buy and gave us detailed instructions for using them. We were intimidated by the gear, but as Aminatou liked to say, "If all these comedy bros can do it, it can't be *that* hard." Then we just called each other up—like one of our usual catch-up conversations—only this time we recorded it. Here's a transcript of the first scintillating moments of our first episode:

> **AMINATOU:** I'm Aminatou.
> **ANN:** I'm Ann.
> **AMINATOU:** Hello?
> **ANN:** Can you hear me?
> **AMINATOU:** Hello?

OK, so there was a learning curve. We are slightly embarrassed when we listen to those early episodes but are really proud that, without hesitation or financial incentive, we committed to showing up and recording the show week after week. (Later, Gina pointed out that the reason the three of us can work together is because we were all the people in high school who would do the group project for the whole group.) We recorded these early rambling episodes in our respective closets at home, and they had a casually intimate tone. After we listened to Gina's first edit of our show, we couldn't believe how good we sounded. Aminatou emailed her, "!!!!!!!! GINA THIS IS SORCERY!!! Delightful sorcery. Wow !!!!!"

Hearing our edited conversation *did* feel like some sort of trickery. Thanks to our casual style, you would never mistake our podcast for an NPR or BBC show, but Gina made us sound good. She cut some of our "ums" and trimmed our digressions, so the conversation flowed quickly from beat to beat. It was the most compelling version of our friendship, translated to audio. The premise was true to life—we really *were* very close friends who, in addition to sharing the details of our everyday existence, spent hours talking to each other about things like the merits of the Squatty Potty, the entrenched sexism of American politics, and the shocking number of scents in Beyoncé's fragrance line. But we didn't mistake the hour we spent recording the podcast every other week for an actual catch-up call. It was a small slice of our friendship, removed from its context and polished up and published.

In the beginning it didn't feel all that different from the frivolous blog we'd started together in the early days of our friendship. In the late 2000s, when we met, it was the dawn of the social-media era and friends made blogs together. Or at least we did. Inspired by our shared sensibility about, well, everything, we opened a WordPress account and started filling our blog with multiple posts a day. Subconsciously we were probably trying to document the inside jokes and cultural references of our early, heady days of friendship before they disappeared from our inboxes and text threads forever. The short-lived blog was a shared mood board, the place where our brains first came together in digital space.

One thing we tell each other a lot is "I love your brain." It's our way of saying, "You're smart, you're clever, I want to hear what you think about everything." From the earliest days of our friendship, we were each fascinated by the way the other organized her thoughts and ideas, and we wanted to know each other's opinion about every single thing. This feeling has never faded away. Even today as we talk to each other, we swear we can feel ourselves sharpening in real time, getting a clearer sense of the world around us and our place within it.

It's no wonder that throughout our friendship we have found ourselves devising ways to hang out with more purpose. Even if we didn't realize it, we were creating excuses to light up each other's minds and jointly focus. We relate to the writer Daniel M. Lavery, who, in his email newsletter, described his friendship with the writer Nicole Cliffe this way: "We have often used work, or the appearance of work, to justify navel-gazing and mutual admiration. We have also often arrived at serious, meaningful realizations about what we mean to one another, what we can give to one another that no one else can, during conversations at least ostensibly ordered around business."

When you are obsessed with your friend's brain, it's natural to crave ordered conversations and excuses to go deeper. And this desire often goes hand in hand with a shared aesthetic or set of values. It's why book clubs are so popular. It's why friends volunteer for charity together or join forces to canvas for a political candidate. It's one reason our '70s feminist foremothers were so into consciousness-raising sessions where women gathered to tell the truth about their lives and connect to each other. It's why in the '90s young radicals collaborated on zines, cutting and pasting drawings and writing in to cheaply xeroxed amateur magazines.

We thought we were making *Call Your Girlfriend* for ourselves and our friends. This was back when podcasts were not something that many people made professionally. So it didn't occur to us that, in putting out our DIY podcast, we were going into business together. Or that we were opening up our friendship to anyone who wanted to listen to and interpret it.

Then our show took off. Within a few episodes, we had a listener base that included way more strangers than friends. Our timing was unintentionally perfect. We launched six months before *Serial* became the first audio megahit and turned millions of people into podcast listeners. Podcasts were a thing now but still so new that there weren't that many of them and definitely not too many made by women. We were featured on iTunes and recommended on magazines' lists of "top new podcasts." Tens of thousands of people found their way to our show—and they became *extremely* invested in our friendship. Because they listened to our podcast on their headphones at the gym or during their commute, they felt like we were a part of their daily lives.

Sure, we had been seen as a close-knit pair by our mutual friends for years, but this was different from attending a wedding together. Lots of strangers who listened to the podcast started following us on social media and occasionally recognizing us on the street. Our listeners took what they heard us say on the podcast and made a lot of assumptions about who we were after we switched off the microphones. Ours became a friendship to aspire to.

Suddenly we had two friendships. We still had our private friendship, the real and sometimes messy relationship that we had been in for years. And now we had a much more public friendship too: an idealized version of our relationship constructed in the imaginations of our listeners, most of whom had never met us. This was like a more intense version of being known as a duo by everyone in our extended friendweb.

But you don't have to start a podcast with your friend in order to experience a disconnect between how easy a friendship looks on the outside and how complicated it actually is. All you need is a social-media account.

If you're relieved that we're *finally* going to talk about how the internet ruined friendship, you are about to be sorely disappointed. Digital communication allows for so many points of connection with a friend, especially one who is physically far away. We honestly cannot imagine being as close as we are today, after years of living on opposite sides of a continent, without the internet.

Digital spaces are how we have all sorts of meaningful one-on-one conversations and private, small-group communication. (Remember, we are still mourning the demise of Google Reader.) In the months after Ann moved away from DC, video chatting replaced our hours of in-person time on the couch and helped us transition to living far apart. We love a story about a long-dormant friendship rekindled with a direct message—and you can pry our group chats from our cold, dead thumbs!—but when people talk about technology as a threat to friendship, they aren't usually talking about private communication. They're talking about social media.

There's a reason adding each other on your social platform of choice has become an important step at the beginning of a friendship. After you've met and felt that spark, but before you've put in the hours and gotten truly vulnerable, adding or following someone can carry the weight of intention: you want them in your feed, you want them in your life. Or you might do most of your messaging on a certain app, so you naturally want to be connected to your potential new friend there. It's no coincidence that when we tell our origin story, part of it includes Ann rushing home to add Aminatou on Facebook—and Aminatou being delighted to find the request waiting from Ann. We already had each other's email addresses, and Ann could have chosen to send Aminatou a private note. Instead, she extended a social-media invitation— which, when Aminatou accepted, was a tiny but concrete way of signaling to the world that we were now friends.

How does digital connection affect friendship? The shortest answer is that it depends. We all use the internet differently. The things that many teens are doing with their phones—like texting or sharing selfies—serve the same purpose and encompass the same "core qualities as face-to-face relationships," according to research from the University of California, Irvine. They are digital actions that build real intimacy. But older people, who have not had a digital component to their friendships for their entire lives, don't report the same benefits. The study's authors speculate that this is because different generations are using different apps, in different ways. Or it could be that older people are using their phones in the same way as teens—leaving comments, sending texts, calling each other with FaceTime—but deriving different meaning from those actions and feeling less fulfilled by them.

It's impossible to generalize, because the expectations of how a friendship should translate to digital space are specific to each friendship. We both have certain friends who love it when we post photos of them online (hey, Daria and Nikki!) because it makes them feel secure in their place in our world. Other friends would consider that same post to be an invasion of privacy. We have some friends who love to seek and give advice via text, offering the details of a problem in a series of paragraph-long messages. We have other friends from whom we never get a text but who always pick up their phone on the first ring. Aminatou has had her phone set on Do Not Disturb since 2012, so Ann is never worried when it goes straight to voicemail. Aminatou always calls back.

Like many friendship rules that go unspoken, it can feel reflexively easy to know how someone prefers to be digitally communicated with. People often set the expectations with their behavior. But if they notice that they're out of sync with a friend, feeling overexposed or neglected or left out, it's important to have an open conversation about it. This is especially true if the friendship is going through a stretch.

In 2015, the researchers Moira Burke and Robert Kraut set out to answer the following question: Does social technology draw us closer to our friends or isolate us? In their review of two studies conducted 15 years apart, they found that the internet's effect depends on how people use it. The studies measured social support, depression, and other aspects of psychological well-being while also taking into account participants' internet use. "The more people talked one-on-one, such as writing wall posts or comments, especially with close friends, the more their well-being improved," Burke and Kraut reported. But the more people looked at strangers' feeds, without that interaction with friends, the worse they felt.

Back when we friended each other on Facebook, the site was mostly a place to keep up with people you already knew in person. But in the 10 years since, social media has shifted—not just the actual sites and apps that people prefer to use, but the ways we use them. Many people follow not only friends but also famous people, semipublic figures, and even the most far-flung members of their extended friendweb. There are more strangers than ever in the average person's feed, which, if you take Burke and Kraut's study seriously, dilutes the potential for actually feeling connected.

And the wider the gap gets between private digital communication *with* a friend and public communication *about* a friendship, the more potential there is for miscommunication and misinterpretation to happen.

We sign off every episode of the podcast with "See you on the internet!" We've been doing that since the early days because back then, even though we had lived in different cities for several years, we were in constant online communication. And thanks to the success of the podcast and the ways the internet was changing, we weren't just seeing each other in text messages and on video chats. We were being seen on social media and making choices about how we wanted to be seen as friends—whether we realized it or not.

Humans have a basic impulse to publicly affirm connections to people we care about. (Many Silicon Valley bros have gotten extremely rich because they've exploited it.) When we post a birthday message, when we thank our friends for supporting us through a tough time, when we designate a hashtag for a group trip, we are creating a digital record of the story we are telling the world about those friendships.

Public displays of platonic affection also help to define our relationship in other people's eyes. "Friend" alone may not connote its importance the way other labels like "brother" or "wife" do. Because we want the world to recognize our Big Friendship for the powerful, important relationship it is, we have had to find ways to talk about it. With the exception of wearing the classic "Best Friends" heart necklace, we mostly do this with our actions, not by literally announcing, "Hello, we are now very close friends. Can you treat us accordingly?"

The two of us like to wear almost-matching clothes. We call it frog-and-toading—when we look like we shopped from the same rack, in the same store, but ended up with slightly difference pieces. We also have matching tattoos—two interlocking circles. When we got them, we cared less about the design itself than about the fact that the same thing would be inked on both of our arms. It's a signal to the world that we are a friend unit.

These friendship-affirming public actions look different for everyone. Some of them happen offline: Friends hold hands when they're walking down the street. They may always show up at parties together. Or keep a very cute photo of the two of them on their desk at work. What they say about their friend to the other people in their social circle is also part of this outward-facing narrative. Any time someone asks about the friend, the answer is part of the story they're telling about that friendship.

But the number of storytelling options we have—and the number of other friends' stories we hear—has changed dramatically thanks to social media.

Sometimes we're not just telling the story of our friendship online; we're writing the headline. In the late 2000s, as Facebook came into widespread use, there was a trend of people changing their status to "in a relationship" with their platonic bestie. For some it was a way of indicating that, despite being single, they had a person they were devoted to. They had chosen each other for this special designation. For others, wary after seeing breakups put on blast with a broken-heart icon, it seemed a safer bet than trumpeting their romantic relationship. Their dating life might be tumultuous, but their best friend wasn't going anywhere. And unlike other ways of digitally signaling your friendship, this one was exclusive. Finally, a way to formally declare your #1 BFF.

The relationship status feature fell out of favor after a few years, but the desire to find concrete ways to show the world which relationships matter to you remains. Posting about friendship is a way of taking something that can be hard to describe — that feeling of being understood by a person you truly love and respect — and making it more tangible. Sure, some people are posing by Instagram-bait murals because they just want to show off that they're on vacation, but for many of us, there's a deeper impulse behind what we post. We want to publicly or semipublicly document our happy moments with friends because life is full of awful things, and it feels good to be able to scroll backward and see a highlight reel of the good stuff too.

N ame a pair of famous best friends. Romantic couples who "married their best friend" don't count, and neither do costars who have been photographed together on a red carpet once. We're talking about people who are *known* for their platonic bond.

Yeah, we said "Oprah and Gayle" too.

Oprah Winfrey and Gayle King are the absolute pinnacle of public friendship. They have, famously, been friends for more than 40 years and call each other four times a day. They have a really good origin story too. Back in 1976, they both worked at a Baltimore TV station, where Oprah was an anchor on the verge of being fired and Gayle was a low-ranking production assistant. One night, a big snowstorm hit, and when Gayle couldn't get home, she had to crash at Oprah's. Gayle didn't have any clothes with her, and Oprah let her borrow a pair of underwear. The rest is friendship history. "We were two black girls who loved being black, who loved the experience of growing up black girls in America, and we felt our value system was very much the same—our dreams were the same," Oprah told the *New York Times*. They also shared a love for Neil Diamond and Barry Manilow.

In an "uncensored" interview about their friendship for *O, The Oprah Magazine*, they talk about the class differences in their upbringings—Gayle's family had a maid; Oprah's mother *was* a maid—and how things could have gotten weird between them after Oprah got rich. One time Gayle, who was not making a lot of money, watched Oprah find $482 in her pocket the way some people would uncrumple a $5 bill. But Gayle appreciated that Oprah never made her feel bad about being less successful, and Oprah appreciated that Gayle never asked to borrow money the way that many other people in her life did. They talk about Gayle going through motherhood and divorce as moments when their friendship was strengthened and affirmed. In 2006, they took a road trip, and while there is video evidence of them getting cranky and annoyed after too many hours in the car together, it ultimately ends with them laughing. From the outside, it seems as though Oprah and Gayle have played everything exactly right and never once faced a friendship challenge so daunting that it threatened to break them.

We're guilty of holding them up as our personal Big Friendship aspiration, our own Shine Theory icons. Oprah and Gayle are the peak. We are mere friendship mortals, gazing upward and devouring every perfect anecdote about them. We love their friendship mythology because it validates our own. They inspire hope. If they could make it through so many years of changes, why can't we? We want to stand the test of time and build side-by-side empires too. We can't wait for whichever one of us is more successful to dedicate a wing of her mansion to the other. (Yes, in Oprah's house there is a "Gayle wing.")

But we find ourselves wondering if it's been all *that* easy for them. Maybe it has been. Or maybe, as their friendship has adjusted to 40 years' worth of stretches and changes, they made a decision to share a few of those details publicly and keep the painful parts to themselves. The point is, we'll probably never know the places where their friendship feels difficult or tender. We idealize a friendship we know almost nothing about.

Oprah and Gayle are an extreme example of a friendship lived in public. But almost every friendship has a version of itself that the people in it project outward, even if the only audience is their immediate circle of mutual friends. Every friendship is subject to interpretation and judgment by outsiders too. And thanks to the internet, there can be a lot of opportunities for interpretation and a lot of people interpreting it at any given time.

Like us, Isaac and Saeed are friends who became colleagues.

For almost two years they hosted a morning show on Twitter. The audience came to know them as a formidable duo: *Isaac and Saeed. Saeed and Isaac.* Their easy rapport and obvious affection for each other makes their relationship easy to idealize: "I love this friendship so much," Isaac told us, "so I love living it out loud." And they are aware of the impact that their friendship has. Saeed explained, "What we're trying to do as friends — as public friends — is to free people." But, he asked, "How do you have a public relationship and also make space for the dents and the rages?" Once, Saeed and Isaac took a road trip for the show they hosted, spending weeks crisscrossing the country in a van together with a video team documenting them. Their audience saw a really fun trip, but their friendship was strained. "We were really struggling because there are limits on how candid you can be in that context, you know?" Saeed recalled. "Doing a damn Wendy's segment or something."

We know this struggle too. At various points, we've had to sublimate what is going on with us, our mental or physical health or the state of our relationship, because we want to remain the sort of professionals who don't drop the ball at work. (Although the podcast began as a side project, it quickly became something both of us considered "work.") We might make passing reference to having a cold or traveling a lot lately, but our show does not track the intimate details of our personal lives. So our listeners hear a polished-up version of our friendship. The easy parts.

In the same way that we can recite the Oprah-Gayle origin story and fill in the rest with our own imagination, serious fans of our podcast knew we met at a *Gossip Girl* viewing party. They knew our years of living long-distance hadn't broken us. They knew that we had seen each other through illnesses and professional ups and downs. They knew a great story about that one Thanksgiving dinner we ate in the parking lot of an Albertsons in Rancho Cucamonga.

But there was so much we weren't telling them. Or each other.

The first years of the podcast were hard ones for both of us personally, in different ways.

Professionally things were going well for Aminatou. She was traveling the country speaking at conferences she used to daydream about attending. Her work was getting big-deal marketing awards and she was on obnoxious tech wunderkind lists. A big tech company came knocking with a job offer that was so good she had to consider it. The role was interesting and challenging. The company was one her father would be proud of and brag about (immigrant child realness). And the pay was more than she ever thought she'd be making: $170,000.

This was the kind of place where you could make yourself a breakfast bowl with quinoa and coconut blossom nectar or eat gourmet monkfish for lunch. All for free! The stock options were generous enough she could start thinking about buying a house. This was a real shot at financial stability and the kind of leveling up she hadn't imagined achieving before turning 30.

This new job also meant moving across the country to San Francisco, and that represented a chance to start over. Aminatou told herself and her East Coast pals that the opportunity was too exciting to turn down, but the truth was that she was nursing a broken heart. For almost a year, Aminatou had been in an undefined romance with a man she had a lot of friends in common with. It was confusing because in private they had a steamy, passionate relationship with intense bouts of fighting and making up, but publicly, they never let on that they were seeing each other. In the beginning, the mystery and sneaking around were fun, but they soon gave way to a lot of frustration. Aminatou uncharacteristically found herself having screaming matches on the sidewalk or leaving restaurants in a huff because of an argument. They were *that* couple.

As Ann listened to Aminatou talk about her growing frustration with the situation, Ann was outraged at how this guy was treating her. *Who does he think he is to treat the best woman in the world this way?* This sounds supportive, but it's actually part of a negative friendship pattern for Ann. When one of her friends is dating someone she thinks is unworthy of their affection, she does this angry-mama-bear thing. She makes *very* clear that she does not like this romantic partner. But even though Ann's reaction is rooted in a protective impulse, her friend does not end up feeling supported. This is what happened when Aminatou tried to tell Ann about her nebulous romance. She felt like Ann was judging her for not extricating herself, and slowly she stopped giving Ann all the details. And so, while Ann knew the contours of what was going on, she didn't know how ugly it had gotten for Aminatou. When Aminatou finally decided to walk away from this person, she felt so lonely. She was breaking up with someone she hadn't even been dating.

Moving to California offered Aminatou a temporary relief, but the reality of her new surroundings quickly set in. That dream job she had moved for? She found out in the middle of orientation that her new team had been reorg'd. That's corporate tech speak

154

for "Nobody cared about the thing that team did so now it's doing something else. Surprise!" The job she was hired to do didn't exist anymore. Would have been nice to know before signing the offer letter and putting all her belongings on a truck across the country. Still, she threw herself into the new role she'd been assigned.

Work was also a good distraction from her deteriorating health. She wasn't sleeping well, and even when she got a full night's sleep, she would wake up in pain and it would take forever to get out of bed. Aminatou was having many Bad Days. The doctors still didn't have concrete answers for her, so naturally she blamed herself "for being lazy" and tried to push herself even harder. She had spent so much time wishing for the life she finally had, and now that it was here, everything still felt hard. But she never wanted to seem like she was complaining.

Finding her place in San Francisco was proving to be difficult too. On an intellectual level, Aminatou knew that the older you got, the harder it was to make friends, but man, does it hit you differently on an emotional level. On most days, she was really proud of how much effort she was putting in to meet new people. Then a cursory Instagram scroll would surface pictures of friends back home all hanging out together, and Aminatou would remember that she didn't have anyone to go to dinner with.

Reminders of Ann hung everywhere in Aminatou's office and new apartment: pictures on the desk and fridge, mementos and cards displayed prominently. Whenever her colleagues or new pals asked about them she would explain who Ann was: "my best friend," supposedly the most important person in her life. What she wasn't telling any of them was that she was barely speaking *to* Ann lately.

Meanwhile, Ann's big-shot executive-editor job had gone down in flames, and she was trying to make sense of what she should do next. The magazine's owners had decided to fire the whole editorial staff—including people Ann had convinced to leave stable jobs and move across the country to work with her. She felt responsible for their unemployment and worried about them landing new jobs. And, for the second time in her career, Ann was working to establish herself as a freelance writer. Just like the first time around, things were extremely financially precarious. But she was starting to get some great assignments and paying her rent with a few weekly writing gigs. Ann yo-yoed between feeling like she was finally living her dream and wondering how long she could make it last.

Ann had also met someone she really clicked with romantically and found herself in a relationship that had possibilities she hadn't expected. This handsome Irishman lived in London, a 10-hour flight from Ann's home in Los Angeles. In a way, this was great for Ann, because it allowed her to maintain her independent life in California while enjoying the thrill of a long-distance love affair, but it was draining the little money that was left in her bank account. By the grace of frequent-flier miles, she was flying to London or hosting him in Los Angeles regularly. Eventually, Aminatou delivered a reality check about how serious things had gotten: "Spending a birthday with someone you're sleeping with means you have a boyfriend."

Some people are really good on the road, able to maintain their community and schedule and strong sense of self no matter what time zone they're in. Ann is not one of those people. And she wasn't just flying back and forth to Europe for the relationship;

she was also picking up writing assignments that required her to travel within the United States too. While both the romance and the work were exciting, the nomadic life was not for her. She was finding it hard to keep up with her friends at home and stay in touch with herself. To make things worse, she had recently gone back on the birth-control pill, which meant she was bursting into tears at random moments, feeling anger and frustration flare up at the tiniest inconveniences, and generally wanting to jump out of her skin.

As the air miles ran out, a decision point loomed for the romance, and Ann was increasingly stressed about it. She looked at the past few years as easily the best of her life, a time when she was super independent, fed emotionally by her friends, and driven by her career. She was enamored of this story of her life, in which Aminatou played a central role. Her new romantic relationship posed a threat to that story. She was either going to have to truly make space in her life for this man, who was willing to move to Los Angeles to be with her, or end things abruptly. Ann agonized over the decision, but she wasn't talking to her friends about it much. And she didn't seek Aminatou's support either. For the first time in their friendship, Ann found herself reluctant to bring up the things she was feeling insecure and sensitive about.

She made the decision to see the romantic relationship through. Which meant her boyfriend was moving to Los Angeles. Which meant he needed a visa. And a new job. The whole thing was extremely expensive and stressful, and it kicked off a period of readjustment for Ann. The last thing she wanted to be was that girl who drops off the edge of the planet when she gets a boyfriend. But this was a time when she was uncharacteristically self-isolated and checked out of all her friendships. And no one felt that more than Aminatou.

But we pushed these feelings down. We had a podcast to record.

W ith the benefit of hindsight, it's easy to see how the gap opened up between our private and public friendships. Social media is designed to encourage posts that either project positivity or provoke outrage. And while we were often outraged about the news, our posts about each other were relentlessly positive and seemingly uncomplicated. We talked about the ways we were proud of each other, selected cute selfies, and modeled Shine Theory. If you'd asked either of us how we felt about our friendship in big-picture terms, we would deliver a speech so full of love and admiration it would bring tears to your eyes. Like that clip of Oprah getting choked up about Gayle.

Those feelings were certainly true, especially at the deepest level. But that wasn't the only experience of our friendship. Publicly, we were not going into detail about where we felt strain. We were not talking about the small misunderstandings and missteps that shook our sense of security and mutual understanding. We described how much we loved all-women getaways like Desert Ladies but not our complicated feelings about gossip or our mismatched expectations about the friendweb. We were talking about race but not about the acute, specific pain it caused in our friendship.

"On social-networking sites such as Facebook, we think we will be presenting ourselves, but our profile ends up as somebody else—often the fantasy of who we want to be. Distinctions blur," writes psychologist Sherry Turkle in her book *Alone Together.* Even if we're trying hard not to fall into the trap, it's easy to adopt the positivity-or-outrage binary of social media.

And when it came to how we both projected our friendship, of course we opted for positivity again and again. Anything in between those two poles felt too personal to put online.

It's fine to deal with friendship strife without blasting it all over the internet. The problem was that we weren't articulating much of the messy middle part offline either. We were finding it difficult to speak freely to each other about the places where we felt hurt or raw. Frankly, it was just easier to cheer for each other, chat about the news, share a superficial laugh. Unite in the fantasy that everything was easy and uplifting in our friendship.

With the podcast doing well, we were selling ads and making money—which meant we had a business. We shared a bank account. We had too many spreadsheets. We had a group text thread with Gina that was a mix of logistical details and memes. We were on the phone several times a week to talk about business stuff, to decide which potential advertisers to approve, to prep for future episodes, or to record. Things were happening very fast, and we felt like we were making decisions by the seat of our sweatpants. While we had long strategized about each other's careers, we had become coworkers practically overnight. And we never paused to acknowledge that's what had happened.

We were now friends *and* colleagues. We started traveling to do events, recording the show in front of a live audience. We had very different reactions to this. Ann liked saying hello to listeners in the lobby after events, but she didn't like sharing herself with strangers on Instagram. She kept her account locked. Unlike on the podcast, where she could be selective about which details of her life to share, she thought of Instagram as a space for her real-life friends. She didn't like the idea of listeners being able to comb through an archive of her photos that hadn't been intended for them. Aminatou, on the other hand, had no problem with listeners following her online, because she had a much greater feeling of control when it came to Instagram. She was, however, skittish about people coming up to her in person. These situations extracted a *lot* of energy from her. She was also uncomfortable with being approached on the street or interrupted at a restaurant, something that didn't happen to Ann as often. These new experiences were stretching both of us, in very different ways.

It's weird to start a business with your best friend. It's also weird to be recognized by a certain niche of strangers as *being* in a Big Friendship. But the weirdest part was that we didn't talk to each other about these things. For the first time in our friendship, we didn't use each other as a sounding board. We just observed how the other person was reacting to these huge changes and assumed she wasn't stressed about our joint business venture or our new status as semipublic figures. We each took the story that the other was telling the world and gave it our own private meaning. And we weren't always right.

If you're not communicating well, the internet offers dozens and dozens of tiny ways you can misinterpret each other. As anyone who has ever agonized over selecting an emoji will tell you, when you're feeling uneasy about a relationship, even small digital actions can take on outsize meaning. And rather than directly ask a friend to clear things up, it's much easier to interpret their digital output. "The problem," Karen North, a communications professor at USC Annenberg, told the *New York Post*, "is that people will 'reach out' by clicking on a friend's page and reading through their posts, and that way they feel engaged even though the engagement was one-sided. So the relationship doesn't actually get furthered, it's just peering into each other's lives."

That feeling of using social media to "peer in" on a friend is not all that different from the experience of keeping tabs on a famous friendship like Oprah and Gayle's. You see only the things they've selected to post publicly, but you tell yourself you know the whole story. Lurking on a friend's social account provides an excuse to avoid the hard, direct conversations that a friendship requires to stay healthy. Digital communication doesn't just offer new opportunities to tell the semipublic story of your friendship. It offers something even more tantalizing: lots of details that you can use as fodder to rewrite the story of that friendship in your own mind.

We still texted each other photos of the grain bowl we made for lunch, quick reviews of whatever TV show we were watching, and many disturbing selfies while we were wearing sheet masks. But our deeper investment in our friendship wasn't keeping pace. *This doesn't feel good, but work is the priority right now*, Aminatou reassured herself. All the hours we were spending on the phone for podcast business allowed Ann to put her head in the sand. *We still talk all the time*, she told herself uneasily.

We both felt the space between us opening up, but at different times and in our own ways. Aminatou was at a party and someone asked her how Ann was doing, and she realized she didn't quite know how to answer. "Uh . . . she's good," she replied vaguely. Ann went to buy a birthday gift for Aminatou and had no idea what to get her. This was troubling, because if Ann is close to someone, normally she has too *many* gift ideas. We would send each other texts like, "I miss you!" Or "We are so due for a long catch-up call." But neither of us was sounding an alarm about how far our friendship was drifting from the way it was projected on the internet.

The real danger doesn't lie in telling a public story about your friendship. It lies in losing your ability to tell the private one. If you're both telling the wider world that you're a friend pair secure in your relationship and hopelessly devoted to each other, how are you supposed to address the fact that friendship is almost always more complicated than that? How do you keep yourself from pretending, even in private, that you know the whole story about each other?

Often, you don't. We didn't.

NINE

Too Big to Fail

W e often told each other that we were "too big to fail."
Too big to fail is a theory that some banks are
so interconnected with the global economy that
their failure would be catastrophic. It was a joke, but we felt it was
true. We shared an LLC, a bank account, and a trademark. We
were known as close friends by the people in our friendwebs; now
strangers who listened to the podcast saw us that way too. If our
Big Friendship failed, we would have to dissolve a professional
partnership that involved Gina, agents, contractors. Emotionally,
failure was even more inconceivable. We'd made it through career upheaval, friendweb drama, and illness together. We couldn't
imagine disentangling ourselves.

Here's the cold, hard truth: "too big to fail" is a lie. We met
in the midst of a recession, so we should have known this. We

watched Bear Stearns go under! (If these words don't mean anything to you, congratulations on avoiding late-2000s financial calamity.) No relationship is too big to fail, and friendship is no exception. We learned the hard way.

In one of the few studies of long-term friendships, researchers surveyed hundreds of adults and found that only 30 percent of their closest friends still remained close after seven years. The study was covered with headlines like "The Seven-Year Expiration Date on Friendships." It's a convenient parallel to romantic relationships, which supposedly experience the "seven-year itch." The term comes from a 1952 play by that name (which later became a movie starring Marilyn Monroe), and the seven-year number referred to the point at which marriages of that generation were most likely to fail. It makes sense. Seven years is long enough to feel like you've already made it through the hard stuff together. Seven years is long enough to develop some really bad communication habits. Seven years is also long enough to feel that the other person should know you well enough they wouldn't do things to hurt you.

Our rough patch came at six years, but we've always been ahead of schedule.

It happened, like a lot of relationship breakdowns, because of what we were going through individually and not communicating about. Our friendship stumbled. Then it kind of wavered for a while, off-kilter. Then it full-on face-planted into the ground. Perhaps this failure, which came after years of security and stability and joy, would have been easier to understand if there had been an explosive incident or deep betrayal to point to, the friendship equivalent of walking in on your spouse in bed with another person. But that's not what happened. It's never as dramatic as you imagine it would be.

Our problems felt highly specific to us and impossible to name. But it turns out that we are the norm, not the exception. The linguist Deborah Tannen, who has interviewed hundreds of women about their friendships, writes that, "Even if a cutoff can be traced to a single moment—a cruel thing said or outrageous thing done—that supremely tellable violation usually is the climax to frustrations and disappointments that had been building over time."

In hindsight, our breakdown seems to have caught up with us in two phases. First, there was a succession of miscommunications and small, seemingly petty moments. Like when Ann invited her boyfriend to dinner thinking that Aminatou could get to know him better, and Aminatou thought Ann brought him as a buffer because she didn't want to have one-on-one conversation. None of these things were devastating on their own, but the bad feelings started to accumulate, making us more reluctant to confide in each other.

Once we stopped being able to talk about the deep, difficult stuff in our lives, we moved on to a new terrible phase in which we began to repeatedly, inadvertently hurt each other's feelings. It became a cycle: Aminatou thinking Ann wasn't upset or bothered by anything, Ann thinking Aminatou was upset with her but being unable to figure out why. We were unintentionally gaslighting each other.

We were no longer speaking the same language. Often, when

Ann thought we'd had a perfectly pleasant interaction, Aminatou felt awful about it, and vice versa. Neither of us ever said to each other, in the wake of a specific painful incident, "This hurt me," or, "I'm in my feelings about this." Instead we were hiding in indirect statements that were easily misinterpreted and each spinning narratives to ourselves about what the other was going through. *What did she really mean by that? Why would she do something like that? She must really not give a shit about me anymore.* We were both cagey and self-protective, too scared and proud to be direct with each other about what we were feeling or what we needed.

This is yet another pattern that crops up in a lot of friendships. In her book *You're the Only One I Can Tell*, Tannen explains that a difference in conversation style—or each person's unique way of saying what they mean and interpreting what another person is saying—is often the invisible culprit when trouble arises between friends who are women. That's because, in many cultures, women are socialized to be less direct, saying things like, "Do you think it's cold in here?" rather than "I'm cold. Would you mind turning up the heat?" Women are also socialized to prize communication as a way of feeling intimately connected. It was certainly true for us that when we stopped being able to communicate, our intimacy broke down. Our shared secure base and safe harbor disappeared slowly, without us noticing until they were gone.

No wonder we couldn't see it. In the easy-breezy early days of our friendship, our conversation styles seemed so in sync, we didn't appear to have separate styles at all. We simply knew which personal questions were OK to ask and which would be received as prying. We knew how to indicate we were paying attention to each other. We knew how to express concern and how to receive the other person's concern too. We could convey deep emotions like solidarity or empathy or fear with the briefest of text messages. We knew how to interpret vague statements and even silences. We just *got* each other. But because we'd never been forced to articulate what was working about our communication, now that it had broken down, we couldn't figure out how to get it back. We avoided talking about the problems that we could both feel but couldn't yet name.

We each retreated to our own corner and interpreted the other's silence in our own way, becoming even more reluctant to share things with each other. "The extreme form of indirectness is silence: communicating meaning by saying nothing," Tannen writes. "That's a tactic that many women use to avoid conflict." (Men do this, too, of course.) The silence between us seemed to grow and grow as our low-drama ethos was finally revealed for the conflict-avoiding behavior it was. In private we had never felt more apart. In public we were performing a friendship that strangers idealized. The podcast was doing well, which is a real testament to our professionalism, our stunted emotions, and Gina's loving cocoon. Queens of compartmentalizing! But on many occasions we felt like frauds hosting a show "for long-distance besties everywhere" when our own long-distance relationship was hanging by such a thin thread. We just soldiered on and told ourselves that we didn't want to let our personal issues interfere with what was now a working relationship. Privately we both started to worry that the podcast was the only thing keeping us together.

Tannen notes that entrenched silence can lead to a phenomenon she calls "complementary schismogenesis." It's what happens when two people end up communicating "in ways they normally wouldn't, as each reacts to the other by increasing the very aspects of their styles that differed in the first place." You think you're trying to bridge the gap by modeling how you'd like to communicate, when in fact you're retreating further from the person you're trying to connect with. Tannen gives the example of two women, Noelle and Tara. Noelle wishes Tara would speak more softly in public places, and so Noelle models the behavior she wants to see, and drops her voice lower. But all Tara hears is her friend speaking too quietly. So she raises her voice louder, implying she would like Noelle to speak up. "Noelle ends up practically whispering," Tannen writes, "and Tara practically shouting." It's the opposite effect of what they both hoped to achieve.

Many of the things that bonded us in the beginning had twisted to become points of weakness that now threatened our friendship. We're both proud and stubborn and only at our most vulnerable with a handful of close friends. We're both strong personalities who feel our best when we are honestly expressing ourselves. And this period was all about putting up walls and leaving things unsaid.

Aminatou felt emotionally estranged from Ann, who hadn't been around to discuss her heartbreak, to strategize about the new job and health woes, or to hear the funny San Francisco observations she had. And Ann, who had trusted Aminatou's guidance through so many of her crises in the past, felt totally unmoored without her. At times Ann thought that if she could just bridge the gulf between her and Aminatou, all the other big changes she was going through would stop feeling so stressful. Ann suspected that this phase of her life wasn't difficult because she was moving in with a boyfriend or trying to shift her identity from "single and loving it!" to "in a happy, stable romantic partnership" but because of the painful day-to-day toll of living without her best friend.

We didn't say these things aloud to each other. We both blamed the other for our emotional stalemate, telling ourselves, "I'm putting myself out there. Why isn't she?" Somewhere, Deborah Tannen is screaming, "Complementary schismogenesis!"

At separate moments, we each recognized we had a problem and tried, in our own clumsy way, to address it. Our emails reflect how much we felt we were walking on eggshells. After Ann returned home from a reflective period away on a writing retreat, she emailed Aminatou, "I have been thinking about you a lot. Several of the women on the retreat asked about my tattoo, and answering their questions made me realize how grateful I am to have a physical reminder that I always want us to be part of each other's lives." Aminatou replied within a few hours: "I've been thinking a lot about you too and how to move on (so ~dramatic~) and I know we'll be OK. It will look different but change is good right?"

In that email exchange, we were acknowledging there was a problem between us that we both wanted to solve. And that acknowledgment, in and of itself, felt like some sort of progress. We thought all we had to do to fix it was to rewind and pick up where we had left off.

W e didn't articulate it this way at the time, but we tried to salvage our friendship by repeating the steps we'd gone through to build it in the first place: trying to find a spark, putting in the face time, and getting vulnerable with each other. This time around, it was much harder.

The days of living a few blocks away were long gone, and every in-person interaction had to be planned and invested in. We were in constant digital contact, which was great for sending each other memes and hot Keanu pics, but texting is an impossible medium for the hard emotional conversations we knew we needed. And we weren't sure we still had spark—at least, not in a positive sense. The only thing we were sparking lately was negative feelings as we misunderstood each other.

But we both still really wanted to fix our friendship. Remember, we swore we were "too big to fail." At this point we had our doubts, but we were really hoping we could make it work. We still cared for each other deeply and wanted to do better.

In an attempt to break the cycle, we landed at a natural conclusion: we just had to put in more time together. That's how we ended up at the spa, trying to save our relationship.

On that spa getaway, we went through the motions and tried to open up to each other. But what really stands out is the uneasy silence, awkward pizza dinner, and stellar body treatments. If you're going to take a sad save-the-relationship vacay, we highly recommend a hot-springs spa. You can't exfoliate the defensive layers around your cold, cold heart, but your outer epidermis will be so soft.

The contrast between that trip and our earliest do-nothing-on-the-couch extended hangouts was palpable. We had both felt hurt for so long that of course we couldn't meet fresh, as if it were the first time. When we got back to our respective homes, it didn't feel like anything had changed between us. The walls were still up.

At the lowest points in our friendship, when Aminatou couldn't sleep, she would start to think of the mechanics of how things would end. *OK, we'll probably have to talk about it. Ugh, we're both so bad about talking about this. We'll have to cancel the podcast and dissolve our LLC and there is so much paperwork to do. Ugh, I hate paperwork. We'll also probably have to talk to all of our other friends about it. I really can't bear doing that. And even then, what does it mean? It's not like I'll never see Ann again. If I see her at a party, will we not speak to each other? That will probably destroy me.*

We know our breakdown could have just as easily ended in a breakup, because we both spent many hours contemplating that possibility. With other friends in our respective pasts, we've had our fair share of temporary situationships, once-close bonds that petered out, and abruptly painful cutoffs. The possibility of a breakup was the specter that haunted our rough patch. The truth is that friendships collapse all the time. They work well in a certain context, and then end when that context changes and one or both people outgrow them. One friend stops stretching, the other friend stops reaching out, and soon they haven't spoken in six months . . . or six years.

For many friendships, that makes sense. People change. Emotionally, though, it's harder to accept the fact that every friend we make might not be a friend forever—especially when only one person wants the relationship to end. There is a catch-22 at the heart of many friendships. We expect the important ones to last forever (hence that last *F* in "BFF"). At the same time, we're taught that if a friendship isn't working, it's perfectly acceptable to walk away—sometimes without even a conversation acknowledging it.

One person can't unilaterally decide to fix a friendship. Repair is a choice that *two* people have to make. We feel extremely lucky that we were both willing to work on our problems, because we know that's not the case in many friendships. The people who listen to our podcast hear us talk about friendship a lot, and so our email inbox has become a repository for one-sided breakdown stories. Who better to tackle sticky friendship questions than us, two people who were supposedly in a *very solid friendship*? If you're shaking your head, know that we are laugh-sobbing with you. And although we've often found ourselves at a loss for how to answer these emails, the stories made us feel less alone in the months when our own friendship was on the rocks. Here's a taste:

> *I think one of my best lady friends has dumped me. We used to see each other all the time, chat constantly on WhatsApp—all the usuals. I felt closer to her than basically anybody. Then in November she started getting pretty serious with her boyfriend and in the months since has slow faded from my life.*

> *I told her I wasn't OK with being treated like that; I was still hurt and needed more time to recover. I left the door open*

for her [to] work on repairing the relationship, but she re-plied with an insult-ridden email that I will paraphrase as, "I SAID I'M SORRY, BITCH."

After a conversation on the phone I initiated to try to find out why she had been blowing me off recently, she let ev-erything out. Berating me for offences she's kept in for up to 10 years. After a string of insults from her and lots of tears and apologies from me, she ended our friendship, stating it was over. And now here I am. A crying mess for the last few days, mourning the loss of a friendship that was part of the center of who I was.

I feel terrible for shutting [my friends] out of my life, and I hated not being a part of their lives for the past few months. But I'm also trying to practice standing up for what I need in relationships.

We've seen emails about all kinds of friendships that have recently been pronounced dead. The slow fade. The never-resolved blowout fight. The long-simmering resentments. The one-sided decision to just move on. Each category comes with its own set of questions. Has the friendship truly run its course, or are you just blowing it off in favor of a new relationship? Are you asking for too much, or are you simply standing up for your own needs? What's the statute of limitations on a friendship transgression? Are you being poisoned, or are *you* the toxic friend? Usually these are questions people are trying to muddle through on their own, not in dialogue with the friend who's prompting them.

In a romantic context, it's not OK to dump someone with a terse text message if you've been going out for several months. And most people agree that ghosting—simply fading away without returning calls or texts—is insensitive, if common. But there are no such rules or formulas for an appropriate friend-breakup. The expected course of action, even if you've been close friends for years, is to disappear from each other's lives, as if it always happens naturally and painlessly.

In fact, friendship fades are often one-sided, more akin to ghosting than a mutual slo-mo abandonment. When one person drops the friendship, the other half of the duo is left wondering whether their friend has fully abandoned them for good or is just kind of busy right now. And even when the reality settles in that the friend isn't coming back, a lot of questions remain about what, exactly, went wrong.

Often, the person who left feels they're finally rid of a friend who wasn't adding anything to their life anymore—or was actually poisoning it. Dr. Miriam Kirmayer, a clinical psychologist and friendship expert, hears a lot of one-sided breakup stories. While Kirmayer is open to helping a pair of friends work through their problems, so far she has treated only clients who come to her alone to process their issues surrounding a friendship. She encounters the idea of the toxic friend frequently in her line of work. "Whenever I'm doing a workshop or giving a lecture, that seems to be the topic that resonates most," she says.

Everyone has had a toxic friend. Just close your eyes, and you can picture this person in all their dramatic glory. Ending a friendship due to toxicity makes a lot of sense—all healthy adults know that boundaries are important, right? But Kirmayer cautions her clients to rethink this construct. She says that people use the word "toxic" to refer to many different kinds of friendship situations, and they don't all warrant the label. "In reality that just kind of obscures the fact that conflict is inevitable in any relationship, including a friendship," Kirmayer says. "Especially a close friendship."

Some friendships really *are* bad for you, but it's also true that people can be too quick to passively say "we grew apart" when they simply stopped putting in effort, or to apply a term like "toxic" to a friendship that might actually be worth saving. "A lot of the work that I do is helping people think a little bit more flexibly, of not seeing that as the only possible or reasonable action to a friendship that is difficult," Kirmayer says. She also pushes her clients to identify patterns in the relationships they're writing off and to take a close look at their own behavior too.

We were both thinking about all of these things as we contemplated whether to walk away from our own Big Friendship. We knew it would mean not only rewriting our expectations for the future but also questioning everything we felt about our friendship in the past. *Were we really as close as I thought?* And there was certain to be a feeling of exposure too. *Someone who knows so much about me has no obligations to me anymore.*

It's hard to rationalize away a friend breakup. You can't blame a fizzled-out sex life or an attraction to a new partner. There's not even the classic half-hearted consolation of "We can still be friends" to fall back on. And so friend breakups can cut even deeper than romantic ones. "We feel almost all the time that no, no, this says something about me—not just as a friend, but me as a *person*," Kirmayer says.

This is why friendship failures are so hard to talk about. They're cloaked in shame and confusion. In her book *You're the Only One I Can Tell*, Tannen says the most gut-wrenching stories she heard were about women's friendships that ended abruptly. "When someone you've been close to, who has been part of your life, suddenly refuses to see you or speak to you, her departure leaves a hole in your life and your heart, and can leave you wondering what you did to cause your abandonment," she writes. "You may suspect that you harbor within yourself a fatal flaw that renders you unfit for friendship."

As one of our listeners wrote to us about the sudden end of her friendship, "I feel worse than any breakup, any job loss, and any family death I've experienced." When a romantic relationship ends or a relative dies, it's acceptable to take some time off work, to spend full weekends in your pajamas, to expect the people in your life to treat you with extra gentleness. But just try calling your boss to announce you've experienced a devastating friend breakup and need to take a day off to grieve. It's impossible to imagine. When a friendship falls apart, the response tends to be more like, "Well, maybe it was time for things to end." That makes the breakup feel even worse.

"With friend breakups, first of all, I think they should be treated seriously," says Kayleen Schaefer, author of *Text Me When You Get Home*. "And, you know, if you're bummed about it, and your other friends don't want to talk about it, you have to let them know how much this is upsetting you. Because if you can't talk about it then you're not going to be able to process it."

And you're going to need to process it. Acknowledging friendship's potential to be one of the deepest and most powerful relationships of our lives also means acknowledging something far more difficult: that its end can cut so deep that the scars might never fully heal. This is part of the beauty in deciding to enter into a Big Friendship in the first place. You're taking an emotional risk. And it's an even bigger risk than people take when they fall in romantic love, because there are so few rules to guide you through the difficult times. There are no rituals to help you heal and move on if the friendship falls apart. And that, Kirmayer says, "can really prolong and intensify the heartache that people feel when it comes to friendship breakups."

The bigger the friendship, the more painful its end. As toxic as our own friendship felt at some points, even worse was the thought of being caught somewhere together, years after we'd broken up, with that terrible "Somebody That I Used to Know" song playing in the background. That would have been hell. And our friendweb was so knit together it was pretty much guaranteed we would keep bumping into each other in person and online, popping up in each other's feeds as a reminder of what we'd lost.

Despite feeling like we'd repeatedly failed to fix things between us, we weren't ready to break up yet. We each had our own reasons we felt our friendship was worth fighting for. Aminatou was racked with the anxiety that the state of the friendship said something deeper about her and her own inability to communicate. *What is it about me? Am I broken?* are questions she asked herself repeatedly. Maybe someone else had answers. Like Aminatou, Ann was questioning herself: *Am I actually just a bad friend?* And the stakes were high. As Ann scribbled in her journal and repeatedly went over the details in her head, the thought she kept coming back to was, *It would be so difficult to leave. It's going to be difficult to stay and fix things too. If it's painful either way, why not stay?*

We each had our reasons, but we arrived at the same conclusion: we couldn't give up on each other yet.

There's an expectation that friendship is the easy part of life. All support, no strife. If it gets hard? Well, it wasn't meant to be. While there are piles and piles of books to help you through a crisis in your marriage and offer you advice on repairing estranged family relationships, not much guidance exists for best friends who can sense things falling apart but don't know how to put them back together. Our Google searches for "help I think my friend is breaking up with me" brought more anxiety than answers. We found a lot of articles about how painful friend splits can be, and almost all of them carried an overwhelming sense of fatalism, as if this were the only natural outcome for a friendship on the rocks.

But how do you go about *saving* a friendship? An extremely chipper wikiHow entry suggests, "Fortunately, you can revive a dying friendship by reaching out to your friend and showing them you care. If you've had a fight with your friend, apologize for your role in the fight and talk things out. Additionally, help your friendship grow by making new memories with your friend and learning to compromise." The illustration is two somber-looking people on a couch.

This lack of resources is flat-out ridiculous when you consider that friendship can be one of life's most important intimate relationships. Sure, some "friends" are just former classmates you struggle to keep up with or people you see for dinner twice a year. Maybe they are easy to forget. But we're talking about real friends. *Big* friends. Friends who know your worst shit and have stuck around anyway. Friends who have seen you grow and change and heard you tell your stories over and over. If intimacy is what makes family and romantic relationships both so rewarding *and* so complicated, why would it be any different for a Big Friendship? When two people entangle their emotional lives, it's bound to be difficult sometimes. Not all friendships look the same for the long term, but one thing is guaranteed: any Big Friendship will face existential threats.

We can't believe we never considered this! Our "too big to fail" hubris is stunning, really. So when we found ourselves in a period of emotional estrangement that we couldn't seem to get out of, we felt a lot of things. Shame. A desire to run away. A desire to just wait it out and hope it got better. Frustration. Confusion. A lot of hurt. We had so many feelings. What we didn't have was a way forward. We didn't know what it looked like to fight for a friendship. We would have to make our own way through it.

And we realized we couldn't do it alone.

A common thing at weddings is to have the friends and family in attendance say their own "I do" and pledge to help the couple make it through the tough times. But for us, the fact that we shared a community made things harder in this difficult phase, not easier. Because our friendweb was so interwoven, we didn't want our honest attempts to resolve this communication breakdown to be perceived as gossip. We didn't want to go to any of our mutual friends for support, because we didn't want them to feel like they had to take sides. That led to both of us turning things over and over in our own heads, spinning out over perceived transgressions without a reality check and feeling ever more isolated as we tried, alone, to figure out the problems that had grown between us. Our journals from this period are a hot mess.

The fact that we worked together is what eventually created the opening for things to start getting better. While there's not much cultural support for trying to save an ailing friendship, you better believe that capitalist America wants you to save your startup or small business. Our shared professional endeavor made it a lot easier to admit we needed help from an expert. As NPR reported in 2015, "Increasingly in Silicon Valley, business partners are looking for help before things go downhill—they're signing up for couples counseling." Cofounders were seeing therapists to smooth out interpersonal conflicts affecting their business. And while we didn't see our problems as work-related, the fact that we were also colleagues gave us enough of an opening to push past the strangeness of going to therapy to save a friendship.

One day, we had scheduled a call to discuss Shine Theory business. Our concept had gotten popular enough that people were starting to ask, "Where's the Shine Theory book?" In some ways, a book seemed like a logical next step for this idea. Neither of us was sure we had the emotional capacity for it.

On the phone call, Ann seemed cagey, and after Aminatou pressed her about it, Ann admitted, "I feel awful." Maybe because we were talking on the phone, this created a different sort of opening than all the emails and text messages we'd exchanged in which we gingerly admitted our friendship wasn't in great shape. We were out of practice in having a real conversation, but we did manage to agree on one thing: we weren't sure how to find our way out of this. We had already tried and failed to "get the magic back" with our hot-springs weekend. Things had been bad for long enough that we knew they weren't just going to get better on their own.

Then Ann suggested we try seeing a therapist together. Hearing this from a dyed-in-the-wool Midwesterner who had never been to therapy, Aminatou knew the suggestion was serious.

That's right. We went to couples therapy.

From the moment we agreed to do it, we were both committed. We coordinated to email a few people we knew to get recommendations of therapists. We decided on a few criteria for what we wanted: A person of color or someone who had strong experience with nonwhite clients. Someone who had feminist leanings. Someone who immediately understood that ours was a platonic relationship, and was not going to confuse it for a romantic one or a mere business partnership. Someone who was willing to work with us remotely, because we still lived far apart. We found someone whom we saw for a few sessions, but leaving his office one day when we happened to be together, we turned toward each other in the elevator and both said it out loud. This guy was not the right fit for us. We started the search process all over again.

A friend recommended a therapist she knew who practiced Emotionally Focused Therapy, a short-term approach (usually eight to 20 sessions) to repairing intimate relationships. Ann googled this and was like, *Omg it's a multistep program.* She felt hopeful. This was curable! Someone had a plan! We would meet regularly for 75- or 90-minute sessions to unpack our emotional baggage.

Our new therapist suggested that we start off with a few in-person appointments, so Aminatou came to Los Angeles for a while. Neither of us had insurance that reimbursed therapy. The sticker shock was real, but we were committed to doing this and decided the money was an investment in our relationship.

For the first few therapy sessions, we met at Ann's house to drive there together. We don't know why we were surprised that sometimes our outfits matched. We made sure we had both eaten, because we can't do emotional work on an empty stomach, and doubled-checked we each had our water bottles. If strangers saw us on the street, they probably would have assumed we were off to do some strenuous exercise, and they wouldn't have been wrong.

At those in-person appointments, we sat awkwardly side by side in our therapist's office and avoided looking at each other. Sitting across from us, the therapist pointed out that we were both there because we still had so much love between us. The bulk of the work, in the beginning, would be to figure out how we were hurting each other and what we weren't telling each other. Ann's newbie optimism about this being a concrete plan for relationship repair started to dissipate. (Aminatou, who was far more experienced with therapy, politely declined to call the therapist by her first name until we'd had a breakthrough.) We had spent so many hours estranged from each other, we were going to have to spend at least as many getting close again.

The sessions began paying off as our therapist started to show us where the cracks in our relationship were. She explained that the cycle we were caught in was one that can undermine any intimate relationship. Ann is a slow processor who might not look like she's emotionally reacting in real time, but she will spend hours reflecting on things. Aminatou appreciates a more immediate acknowledgment that something difficult has transpired, and feels the best when there is a clear plan and timetable for following up. Thanks to these big differences between us, and others that we had previously failed to see, our attachment had broken down. We were no longer each other's secure base or safe harbor, which is why we were reluctant to get vulnerable with each other. And why, despite us both wanting desperately to reconnect, we felt completely unable to. At one point, our therapist looked like a satisfied detective who'd cracked the case when she spelled out our destructive emotional pattern: Ann was so afraid of hurting Aminatou that she was holding back. And Aminatou, sensing Ann was withholding, moved further away herself. Ann, who could tell that Aminatou was moving away, figured she had done something to hurt her and backed off even more. "And that's why it's called a cycle," our therapist said.

The payment machine in the parking garage near our therapist's office had a quote prominently displayed above it: "Success is how high you bounce after you hit bottom—George Patton." Leave it to a warmonger to accurately describe our battle for emotional reconnection. Even on the hardest days, we still managed to laugh at it every time we left the garage.

Therapy saved this relationship by giving us a space where we could talk about our individual shit with a certified adult in the room and learn to deal with it together. If you've been to therapy you know that so much of the process is the therapist repeating to you things you have said. "What I think I am hearing you say is . . ." is a sentence construction that still makes Aminatou shake. It's powerful to have your thoughts echoed back to you. Sometimes the therapist was right on the money, and other times we struggled to explain ourselves further. For two people who are obsessed with putting ideas into words, it was clarifying for each of us to hear where we agreed or where we were failing to convey how we felt. Our therapist would often make us turn to each other and articulate feelings we thought were obvious.

"I am afraid to lose you."

"I thought I had already lost you."

We couldn't believe how many big, important things—like needs and expectations and preferred modes of relating to people— we'd never explicitly discussed with each other. Much of the therapy process was about undoing our powerful story of sameness. We had to be shown how different we really are before we could start to understand our actions. We had made so many assumptions, most of them going back to the ease of our earliest days of friendship. And we are still learning how to un-assume them.

Among our friends, everyone seems to have a therapist. We know a ton of people who have been to therapy with a romantic partner. We know a few people who have been to family therapy too. But going to couples therapy with a friend seems . . . out there. Radical and extravagant. We did not tell many people we were doing it.

It still seems weird to say, "We went to therapy to save our friendship." But it doesn't sound so ridiculous when the flip side could easily be "We didn't do everything we could to save our friendship." What's incredible about friendship is that it allows you to be non-exclusively immersed in another person's reality, to be intimately known by someone in a way that's separated from the whims of sexual desire and the constraints of family. It's a beautiful mix of independence and dependence, something you both have to continually opt in to. And these are the exact things that are likely to tear it apart from within. If every friendship is governed by its own unspoken agreements, when circumstances inevitably change and render the old agreements useless, the only way to evolve is to rewrite them, explicitly. That's what we did and what we're still doing.

We know therapy is expensive, and we don't take for granted that this was even an option for us. At an earlier phase in our lives we definitely wouldn't have been able to afford it, let alone emotionally go through with it. But this was our way of committing to actually doing the work with each other, not just saying we were open to it. It was our way of investing—literally—in our friendship. Maybe some Big Friendships can be saved by a weekend getaway and some good intentions. But not ours. We couldn't get there on our own. We needed a professional intervention, and we're actually extremely proud of ourselves for figuring that out.

Now the most heartbreaking thing isn't that we had a rough patch or that we hurt each other and miscommunicated for such a long time. The saddest part is the time we'll never get back. The moments we missed in each other's lives during that period. The hard stuff we weren't there for, the inside jokes we never created, and all the ways our friendship might be different if it had never broken down.

The good news is we're still here. We're still big. We just know how much work it takes not to fail.

..

TEN

The Long Haul

W e're now a full decade past our meet-cute. We've lived apart for more than twice as long as we lived in the same city. We still see a lot of each other and talk almost daily, although those years of watching TV on the couch or lingering at happy hour every week feel very far away. The truth is that it's harder for us to fit into each other's lives than it once was—and we *work* together.

In recent years, most of our friends have seen their personal and professional responsibilities expand. Time has never felt more precious or scarce. The experts say that, when it comes to friendship, ages 30 to 50 tend to be a low point. It's a time when spending unstructured hours with friends, an activity that feels second nature when you're younger, starts to seem luxurious. Or even indulgent. If you're lucky, like we were, you have a lot of time for friends in young adulthood. Those friends help you figure out who you are, who you want to be, and what you need to ask from the world. And then, when you finally start to feel at home in your identity and fulfilled in your aspirations, you barely have time for the people who helped you get there.

In a *New Yorker* essay published the year we met, the humorist David Sedaris wrote about the "four burners" theory of life priorities. He learned this metaphor from a woman he considered successful and happy. The woman explained that life was like a stovetop: "One burner represents your family, one is your friends, the third is your health, and the fourth is your work." In this metaphor, your stove can't run for long with all four burners going. In order to be successful, you have to switch off one of the burners. And if you want to be *really* successful, you have to pick just two to keep lit. Few of us have the luxury of switching off work. For many people, switching off family is unthinkable. And switching off health is unsustainable, to say the least. So, for most people, the "friends" burner is the first to go.

The stove metaphor might describe how some time-strapped adults think of their lives, but it only takes into account your energy output, not what you *receive* in return from each of these important areas of life. Although the metaphor makes it seem very clear, our lives are not as easily separated into pots that can be placed on separate burners. Extinguishing friendship has consequences for every other aspect of life. Without Shine Theory, it's harder to keep your work burner lit or find support when you're leveling up professionally or suffering a setback. Without friends, it's much harder to get through periods of family transition, like the death of a parent, the arrival of a baby, or an estrangement from a sibling.

As for health, friendship has a bigger impact on a person's psychological well-being than their family relationships. Its absence has physical consequences too. "During my years caring for patients, the most common pathology I saw was not heart disease or diabetes; it was loneliness," wrote former surgeon general Vivek Murthy in the *Harvard Business Review*. "Loneliness and weak social connections are associated with a reduction in life span similar to that caused by smoking 15 cigarettes a day." He went on to list various other negative effects of social isolation. It's not just doctors who are concerned. In 2018, the UK government appointed a minister to address loneliness, and Australians called on their leaders to do the same.

Loneliness is not the condition of just being alone. A more accurate definition, according to the *Washington Post*, "is the distress people feel when reality fails to meet their ideal of social relationships." In other words, lonely people don't necessarily lack friends. Even as concern about "the loneliness epidemic" has increased, the percentage of Americans who say they have no friends has remained consistently tiny, in the single digits. Maybe more people are lonely because they aren't making time to stay connected with those friends in a meaningful way, over the long term. And social media is playing a role, allowing them to "peer in" at people they once truly felt connected to and opening up the gap between their wishes for those friendships and the more anemic reality: that those friends are not fellow travelers who are sharing their ups and downs, their joys and sorrows. They are friends in name only.

The researcher William K. Rawlins puts friendships in three categories: active, dormant, and commemorative. The active ones are important bonds in your life right now. You are investing in these friends by spending time with them, you know about the day-to-day details of their lives, and you probably see them fairly often. This is the category that Big Friendships fit into. The dormant friendships are ones that were once active but for reasons of circumstance aren't going strong in a daily way. With dormant friendships—which is probably the category most associated with the dim back burner—there's the perception that they could be resurrected at any moment, when you'll just "pick up where you left off." Finally, there are commemorative friendships, ones that have ended abruptly or faded away, and you don't expect to ever come back to. It's easy to see how someone could feel lonely if they have friends only in the dormant or commemorative categories.

You're allowed to rewrite the rules of a friendship and shift categories at any time. Sometimes the new rules are implied, when one or both of you experiences a big life change that reshuffles your priorities, and you stretch and readjust your expectations in tandem. But sometimes it's a one-sided shift from active to dormant, and especially if you've never talked about it, you can't be sure that the friendship will still be there waiting when you're finally ready to rekindle it. As anyone who's taken time out of the workforce to be a full-time caregiver knows, it's not always easy to switch a burner back on after it's been extinguished for a long time.

Perhaps a better question is, how do you prevent a friendship from getting cold?

When things in our friendship were at their worst, Ann would lie awake in bed, and like Aminatou, she would spiral into dark thoughts about how we'd never be close again. In those moments, Ann often consoled herself with an image: her and Aminatou, decades into the future, bumping into each other at some professional event or mutual friend's retirement party. (As if anyone in our generation is ever going to retire.) In this vision, we didn't mend things in our 30s, and we have grown further apart. Decades have gone by. Old Aminatou has kind of a Toni Morrison vibe—cheekbones as sharp as ever—and Old Ann looks like a cartoon librarian. We are both wearing the kind of comfortable, flowing linen garments we have already begun to favor. (The Eileen Fisher years come at you fast.) But now, with the benefit of advanced age, the resentment and awkwardness have magically melted away. We sneak away from the event together, and over a long meal, maybe followed by a few strong cocktails of the sort we rarely indulge in anymore—daiquiri for Aminatou, dry gin martini for Ann—we give each other the real update on all the things we've missed out on in the intervening years. We would feel that closeness, or the possibility of it, the same way we did in those first few months of our friendship. Enough time has passed that we can become obsessed with each other again. Only we're now older, wiser, more aware of what really matters. An absurd fantasy!

It's tempting to think that we'll get to a certain point in life— 10 or maybe 20 years in the future—when we'll have it all together. When we'll feel confident in our careers, completely secure in our sense of self, and fulfilled in our relationships. No more communication missteps. No more ignoring our problems by getting high and binging some TV. A perfectly decorated home that we own. Robust savings accounts. The ability to instantly repair long-broken or neglected friendships with a single night of conversation.

In the earliest phase of our friendship, our ideal was to stay close to each other forever, without a whiff of strife between us. The goal was to reach Oprah and Gayle status, effortlessly walking the line between depending on each other and being fully independent women. Our friendship would always be a refuge of support and love and hilarious elaborate inside jokes, and we would never hurt each other—intentionally or unintentionally.

Some parts of that still sound great, but perfection and ease are no longer our ideals. We're more interested in resilience. Working on our friendship to save it has proven how ridiculous Ann's old-age reunion fantasy was. You can't stay truly connected without some level of misunderstanding or conflict, and you can't get back the years you weren't present for. So the real Big Friendship goal is just to stay in it. Instead of pretending we won't be challenged, we want the ability to bounce back and heal our inevitable wounds.

There is no autopilot mode for a Big Friendship. You just have to keep showing up. Active friendships require active maintenance. You don't get to sit back, do nothing, and enjoy the benefits of a meaningful relationship—any relationship. But action is especially important to friendship, which carries no familial expectations or marriage license. If you don't take action to mark it as important and keep it alive, a friendship will not survive.

Just as there are conditions for creating a Big Friendship, there are also some ways to make sure it stays big over many years. Emily Langan, the professor who applied attachment theory to close friendships, told us that staying attached to a close friend can be boiled down to three main things: ritual, assurances, and openness.

The first, ritual, is because "we need commemorative experiences together," Langan says. This is why families rely on holidays to bring them together and why wedding anniversaries have endured as a way of celebrating the years of investment in a marriage. "Friendships don't have the hallmarks," Langan says. "They don't have the milestones." So it's up to the people in the friendship to create them.

Our friendship anniversary is marked as an annual recurring event on both of our calendars. In previous years, we've sent gifts, gone to dinner, and made time for long phone calls to mark the occasion. You'll find effusive anniversary posts about each other in our social-media archives. We were so busy writing this book that we didn't celebrate our milestone tenth anniversary, but don't worry, we'll do it up right for our 11th.

Even when it's not tied to a special calendar date, an annual getaway with friends is one reliable form of ritual. Traveling to the same point on the globe, especially if you live far apart, is more than a frivolous vacation. It's how all the parties recommit to staying in each other's lives. For all of its imperfections, Desert Ladies is a great example of this. It happens every January, always in the golden light of the Southern California desert. It has food traditions (we order a catering spread called the "Business Lunch" from a Middle Eastern restaurant), private jokes, and a recurring guest list. Ann doesn't feel like the New Year has truly begun until the Desert Ladies trip is complete.

Existing holidays can also be an opportunity for ritual. Aminatou has spent the last couple of Thanksgivings with the same group of friends. They always go somewhere out of the way. She has really come to appreciate, as life gets busier, what a gift it is for the people she loves to take two flights and a three-hour car ride to celebrate holidays together. The menu is different every year, but at the table, they always take turns saying what they're thankful for. It is both a way of catching up on each other's lives and collectively setting intentions for the coming year. Holiday rituals provide families with a sense of identity and belonging. They are a way of transmitting values, history, and culture from one generation to the next, and they can serve the same purpose for friends.

But not all rituals are big events. Sometimes it's the smaller practices you have that remind each other of the importance of your friendship. Aminatou relishes waking up every day to a poem from her friend Sarah. It is a reminder of Sarah's radical softness and kindness, her ability to find something beautiful every day, no matter what is going on in the world. She often tells Aminatou that "soft & lovely is a lifestyle" and now Aminatou knows it's true. Whenever Ann visits her friend Josh—a bestie of more than 25 years—on her first night in town, they go to the same restaurant. And they order the same thing: two veggie burgers with bacon (Ann violating the terms of her vegetarianism is part of what makes this ritual a ritual) and two glasses of the house red. It's a private tiny routine exclusive to that friendship, not just a story she and Josh tell, but something they *do*. Together.

Even when you're separated by many time zones, digital connection allows for rituals too, like always texting each other whenever you're doing a specific thing, or making plans to watch a show at the same time but separately every week. We have a shared Photo Stream with about a dozen far-flung pals, where we post selfies of our outfits any time we feel cute. Multiple nights per week, Ann's high-school bestie Bridget will simply text her, "Good night!" at the end of the day. And whenever she flies, Aminatou sends her friend Shani her flight-tracking information. Shani, who knows Aminatou is a nervous flyer, texts back immediately and gently reminds her, "The plane knows what to do." This makes Aminatou feel seen and comforted. Someone cares that she's in a metal tube, 40,000 feet above land. The ritual also reminds her that she can always count on Shani.

Ritual alone is not enough, though. This is where assurances come in. Even the closest of friends need to assure each other that the friendship is important. Langan says that another key to staying attached is to find verbal and nonverbal ways to tell each other you plan to be there in the future. She offered an example from her own life: "I say to my friend Jill, 'Well, imagine when we're 65. Are we still going to joke about the bad time we had in Cancún?' I'm giving a verbal indicator that I see us as friends when we're 65." It's not exactly a marriage vow, but it hints at a long-term commitment.

And similarly, when the two of us joke about wearing matching caftans and sitting side by side on our *Golden Girls*–style lanai, it's more than a joke. It's an assurance that we plan to be in each other's lives that long. This happens in shorter-term ways too, like when you pick up the check for dinner and tell your friend, "Don't worry, you can get me back next time." One of our biggest assurances to each other was the choice to get matching tattoos, which means we are permanently frog-and-toading. We might never

195

share physical characteristics the way blood relatives do, but we can have matching tattoos, an external sign to the world and to ourselves that we belong to each other.

Sometimes Big Friendship can be assured on a level of paperwork. Most commitments on paper are reserved for family and romantic relationships. Things like marriage licenses, birth certificates, and adoption paperwork have no equivalent in friendship. But there are some ways to declare a friendship in terms that major institutions understand. Years ago, when Ann had a will drawn up, she named Bridget as the recipient of all her worldly possessions. When the lawyer asked her who Bridget was and Ann replied, "My oldest, best friend," his eyebrows shot up. Aminatou designated Shani as her medical proxy, the person who makes health-care decisions for her if and when she is unable to make them herself. In a friendship, this is about as concrete as assurances get.

And finally, we weren't surprised when Langan told us that openness is another important way of staying attached in a friendship. The need for transparency arises when one of you is feeling stretch or strain because of a change that's affecting the friendship. Usually the only way through it is to acknowledge it's happening. And yes, it's hard. Especially if a cold silence has become the friendship norm, initiating a classic discuss-the-relationship talk about the ways you're feeling out of sync in a friendship can feel extremely risky.

"I can call my spouse out on something because the assumption is they have to stay," Langan says. "In friendship there's pretty strong fear of abandonment, fear of loss, because there's nothing holding you in. And so a lot of people are tentative, because you don't know necessarily that the person's going to stay with you. Because they don't have to." Being vulnerable about all the ways you're feeling disappointed or unhappy in a friendship also opens up the potential that your friend is going to say, "You know what? I haven't been present for this friendship because I actually don't want to be in it anymore." And what could be more painful than *that*? No wonder most of us opt for silence and allow the friendship to slide into a dormant or commemorative category.

For us to begin addressing our own friendship-threatening problems, the feeling of our silence had to get so bad that we were sure we had nowhere to go but up. That was what it took to force a transparent conversation. Now it seems pretty clear to us that if we'd never exposed our troubles to the light, they would have eaten away at the friendship until there was nothing left. That's not to say the process has been easy. But we are, as we said to each other in many difficult times, still here for each other.

Langan adds that being transparent also means opening up about how important someone is to you as a friend—making sure you are *saying* to them that you value their presence in your life. Don't just occasionally think of your friend fondly. Tell them that your life would lose meaning if they disappeared from it. Tell them you love them. Tell them exactly why you want to hold on to this friendship and make it last for the long haul.

You don't want a friendship to be resilient just so it endures. You want a big, resilient friendship so *you*, as a human, can be resilient when you're presented with the horrible shit that life will most definitely throw your way. We think of Big Friendship as a way to deepen and diversify the community of support that will see us through the hard times. If you prioritize only your romantic relationships, who is going to hold your hand through a breakup? Relying on your spouse to be your everything will definitely undo your marriage. No one human can meet your every single emotional need. If you only prioritize your kids, what happens when they're grown and living far away, wrapped up in their own lives? Or if you only prioritize work? Wow, that's too sad to even contemplate.

Friendship can definitely survive, simmering on the back burner, in a way that some other relationships can't. But not indefinitely. What's in it for your friend if you are not equally invested? If you tune into the friendship again only after a divorce or once your kid is in preschool? Absence might not make the heart grow fonder. You run the risk of realizing that there's not as much there as you remembered.

We give relationships meaning by the amount of attention and work we put into them. Just as we can choose to leave our friendships unattended and hope they stay warm, we can also choose to elevate our most important friendships to a status equal to marriage, family, and career. We can choose to keep them active, to keep investing in them.

There are big rewards if we do. Friendships become more important as people age, according to a 2017 study—so much so that even the researchers were shocked. "I went into the research sort of agnostic to the role of friendship," the study's author, the psychology professor William Chopik, told *Time* magazine. "But the really surprising thing was that, in a lot of ways, relationships with friends had a similar effect as those with family—and in others, they surpassed them." He noted that, by old age, superficial and circumstantial friendships have faded away. The friendships that last till the end tend to be "the really influential ones"—the Big Friendships.

At the very end, whenever it comes, we will definitely want our friends there. Bronnie Ware, an Australian nurse who spent several years caring for patients in the last 12 weeks of their lives, recorded their dying epiphanies and published a book about it. One of the patients' top five regrets was that they hadn't stayed in touch with their friends. "Often they would not truly realise the full benefits of old friends until their dying weeks, and it was not always possible to track them down," Ware writes. "Many had become so caught up in their own lives that they had let golden friendships slip by over the years. There were many deep regrets about not giving friendships the time and effort that they deserved. Everyone misses their friends when they are dying."

Are you crying? We're crying.

Most of us are going to need the support of a friend long before we find ourselves on our deathbed. "When the universe gives you a crash course in vulnerability, you will discover how crucial and life-preserving good friendship is," the psychologist Harriet Lerner told the *New York Times*. Perhaps unsurprisingly, Lerner is the author of *The Dance of Connection*, a book about how intimate relationships can survive a communication breakdown, that we definitely noticed on our therapist's shelf.

Ann has been bracing for her crash course in vulnerability for years now. In several decades on this planet, she has never experienced the death of a close loved one, true financial precarity, a serious illness, deep emotional trauma, or family estrangement.

For her, this absence of pain only underscores the importance of friendship. It's because of her friends' experiences that she knows just how harrowing life can get, and why she is committed to investing in the people she knows will see her through it. Ann knows the pain is coming for her someday. And when that day comes, she is really going to need her friends.

Aminatou, no stranger to grief and major illness, has had her friends step up for her again and again. They've rushed to ERs on both coasts, stayed by her side, taken notes when doctors were giving instructions Aminatou couldn't quite process, and advocated for her when she needed them. Over the years, her chronic illness symptoms worsened. New ones also appeared, and it was hard to tell if they were connected to each other. She was poring over medical textbooks, looking for answers.

When her new ob-gyn confirmed she had cancer, it was definitely a blow, but she wasn't surprised. In some ways it was a relief to have a name for this collection of symptoms she had been feeling for years. Knowing it was endometrial cancer now meant she could focus on making a plan, and that plan would involve asking for help while she underwent treatment and surgery. She leaned on Shani especially hard. Shani would be the person keeping the friendweb updated and was also the person who would take Aminatou to and from surgeries. When Aminatou came to in the recovery room after a long surgery to remove her tumor, the only words she remembers the surgeon saying were "Do you want me to bring Shani in? She's been here the whole time."

Aminatou asked Ann to organize a schedule for friends to drop off food during her surgery-recovery period, and Ann was glad to take the assignment. It was then that Ann felt a new level of gratitude for the hours we had spent in therapy together. She couldn't imagine trying to support Aminatou if the two of us were still emotionally estranged. Even as it was happening she realized that this was one of those big stretches that she and Aminatou had to experience together, otherwise the relationship would never recover. Still, when Aminatou told her not to fly out to be there in person when she was recovering from surgery, Ann couldn't help but wonder if it was because she wasn't as close to Aminatou as she had once been. But she channeled her energy into doing what she could to support her friend from a distance. And with the help of a few of Aminatou's other friends, she organized solidarity blood drives in several cities. Giving blood to help other patients was one thing Aminatou had specifically asked people to do, and Ann wanted to make sure everyone followed through.

Friendship is a real-deal insurance policy against the hurricanes of life—and there's social-science evidence that the hard stuff seems less difficult with a good friend by your side. In one study, participants were asked to assess how steep a hill was. Those who participated with a friend said the hill seemed less daunting than people who participated alone. A Big Friendship can hold you when you're worried that everything else is falling apart. It can be a space of validation when you feel alone in the world. It can provide the relief of feeling seen without having to explain yourself in too many words. And it offers the security of knowing that you won't have to go through life's inevitable challenges alone.

There is tremendous value in having a witness to your singular life. We all want to be understood. And being understood over time is an incredible feeling. Aminatou's friend Antoine once

201

emailed her a sentiment she shares: "I love that you've known every version of me. You were there at the beginning and I want you there at the end."

This is a very old idea that still manages to feel fresh and inspiring. Greek philosophers were obsessed with friendship as an essential virtue and a pillar of the good life. There is, they argued, no pleasure, fulfillment, or meaning without friendship. According to Aristotle, friends hold a mirror up to each other. This mirror allows them to see things they wouldn't be able to observe if they were holding up the mirror to themselves. (We think of it as the difference between a shaky selfie and a really clear portrait taken by somebody else.) Observing ourselves in the mirror of others is how we improve as people. We can see our flaws illuminated in new ways, but we can also notice many good things we didn't know were there. Until a friend specifically requests you bring your lemon meringue pie to brunch, you might not realize you've become an excellent baker. Until a friend finds the courage to tell you that she never feels like you're listening to her, you might not realize this is how others are perceiving your chatterbox tendencies. After the third friend in a row calls you for help asking for a raise, you might finally give yourself credit as a pretty good negotiator. Once you've seen yourself in a mirror of friendship— in both positive and challenging ways—the reflection cannot be unseen.

Our friend-yenta Dayo uses a different metaphor to get at the same idea. "There's a kind of sonar with friendship," she explains. "You're bouncing your personality off things and people so that it's reflected back to you. Good friendships produce true knowledge about yourself, even just subliminally." It makes sense that many of us feel the intensity of our friendships the most when we are young and first forming our sense of self, or in other periods when our identity is undergoing big changes. It also explains why we feel compelled to let go of friends sometimes as our identities shift. Our sonar simply can't find them anymore. Or, to use the Greeks' metaphor, we don't want their mirror. The self we see reflected doesn't suit us anymore.

We feel like we've had a few different friendships in our 10 years. We're still impressed by the women—one fueled by post-breakup pain and the other by solidarity—who lifted a heavy dresser up several flights of stairs. We're still shaking our heads at the two women in their respective closets, thousands of miles apart, trying to figure out how to use their recording devices. We have so much compassion for the women sitting in adjacent mud baths on a "rekindle the magic" spa weekend that failed to revive their flagging friendship. We're proud of the women writing this book, who showed up to work every day to give an honest accounting of their feelings and to understand each other better.

And some things are the same as they have been for a long time. We still have lots of points of connection in our friendwebs. We still practice Shine Theory. We still have to figure out how to talk about our feelings in real time when we don't see each other in person every day. We still stretch for each other. We still make a podcast together, which means we continue to navigate being friends *and* coworkers. We are still repairing our relationship after what Aminatou has referred to as "our emotional Katrina"—an unnatural disaster of epic proportions. But we're still here.

Just as it's hard to remember who we were before we were

friends, it feels impossible to explain the two women we are now. We're embarrassed to admit that, even after writing all these words about our friendship, there is still so much we have to learn about each other. And yet, through this friendship, we have learned more about ourselves, our bad patterns, our capacity for love, and our ability to adapt than through just about any other relationship either of us has had. We're proud we let our friendship get so big, and then fought to keep it big. We can't imagine who we'd be if we hadn't.

It might be true that some rare Big Friendships survive and thrive, strife free, to the very end. No rough patches. Easily switching from active to dormant and back to active again, with no one getting their feelings hurt. But it seems highly unlikely to us. Can you name any deeply meaningful relationships in your life that are 100 percent easy-breezy? We cannot.

Most of us are going to have to work to stay in a Big Friendship. We're going to have periods of stretching to the point of strain, and periods when we really need our friend to do the stretching. We're going to have moments when we feel out of sync. Times when we don't feel understood and seen. Situations in which we feel failed by our friend, and other situations in which we are doing the failing. All the rituals and assurances and openness in the world can't make a Big Friendship feel easy all the time. And when it's hard, the only way for a Big Friendship to survive is for both people to decide it's going to. Showing up, in good times and in bad, is the only way to stay in it.

The upside is you get to be seen for who you really are. You get the security of a safe harbor. You get the satisfaction of knowing that you chose each other and continue to choose each other every day. You get to know yourself deeper than you ever thought possible, thanks to this external mirror in the form of your friend. And you get a *lot* of really good inside jokes.

Not all friendships offer these things. So when you find a Big Friendship that does, hold on to it. Invest in it. Stretch for it. Even when the world is telling you it's *fiiiiine* to let it languish. Even when you're busy. Make a decision to create a world in which Big Friendships are valued as the identity-shaping, life-altering relationships they truly are. Start by valuing your own friendships — not just for their pleasures, but for their challenges too.

We can't tell you exactly what this will look like, because every Big Friendship is different. We can't even promise you that it'll work out in the end and that your friendship will be around forever. We're not even sure about our own. But we can say definitively from our experience: If you take your friendships seriously, you won't regret it. We never have.

Acknowledgments

Welcome, thirsty readers!

Priscilla Painton and Julianna Haubner, thank you for believing in this project from the start, recognizing it as a Big Ideas book, and midwifing it into existence. And to Caitlyn Reuss, Elise Ringo, Hana Park, and the whole team at Simon & Schuster. We are proud to publish our first book with you.

Carrie Frye! Holy shit. We have learned so much from you about how to translate thorny, complex ideas and stories into one coherent thing that people can pick up and read. You are a master of your craft, and we were humbled to be your conjoined acorns. You became our friend in this process, and we are so deeply thankful for you.

Elizabeth Spiridakis Olson, thank you for being on our wavelength and taking care of business. Milan Zmic and De Marquis McDaniels, thank you for making it work.

Acknowledgments

To our earliest readers, thank you for being gentle with our manuscript and generous with your feedback. Your guidance was so valuable, and this book is so much better because you took the time to help us. Jocelyn Hayes Simpson, we love your brain! Thank you for teaching us about "the note behind the note" and pushing us to write the best story possible. Tamara K. Nopper, thank you for your clarity and precision. Brandon Taylor, your advice on separating narrative from ideas and putting it all back together was iconic. Thank god you are teaching the children how to write. And thank you to everyone who supported this book with a blurb, a public endorsement, or a private word of encouragement.

Beth Pickens, you were our cheerleader from day one, and we couldn't have done it without you. Thank you Claire Mazur and Erica Cerulo, Helaine Olen and Harold Pollack, and Glynnis MacNicol for your transparency and generosity in sharing your book proposals and cowriting experiences. Aubri Juhasz, thanks for helping us with research, checking our facts, and navigating our maze of Google Docs. Davis Bynum, thanks for spending so many hours transcribing our interviews and conversations. You know all of our secrets!!

Sarah Sophie Flicker and Jesse Peretz, Michael and Annette Stauning Flicker, Lauri and Doug Freedman, Zara Rahim, and Ruth Ann and Bill Harnisch, thank you for housing us while we were writing this book. Your generosity is life-changing, and we are so lucky to know and be known by you. And thanks to Warren and Beryl for keeping us comfortable and fed in Freeport.

Team CYG, you're the very best! Shout out to Jordan Bailey, Carly Knowles, Brijae Morris, and Laura Bertocci. Quinn Heraty, thank you for protecting our ideas and sending so many stern emails on our behalf.

Gina Delvac, we would be nowhere, absolutely nowhere, without you. We love you for your brilliant brain, your calm action in the face of disaster, your steadfast support without ego. You are the best collaborator we could have possibly hoped for.

Dayo, thank you for introducing us. You just *knew*. We can't imagine our lives without your years of friendship. Thank you for always checking in. Thank you for being an early reader of this book. Thank you for being our forever champion.

AMINATOU WOULD LIKE TO THANK

I can't believe I scammed my way (or was I scammed?) into writing a book.

Jay Mandel, I walked into your office not knowing what an agent was or did, but I left feeling like a lot of my dreams could become a reality. Thank you for always giving it to me straight. I am so thankful for everyone at WME who works behind the scenes to make my life a little easier, especially Sian-Ashleigh Edwards. Doug Singer, I am so grateful for your counsel and your friendship. Deborah McIntosh, my dear friend, thank you for believing in me.

Lauren Shonkoff, thanks for your help when we were selling this book and thanks for your help today. I love money and you keep me paid!

I come from a part of the world where daughters are not always allowed to be full human beings. Both of my grandmothers never went to school and were married off very young. My father made a choice to give me a very different life. Papa, thank you for always taking me seriously. Marly and Alpha, I am really enjoying becoming your friend and I really wish our mom were alive to see it.

It feels both extravagant and deeply embarrassing to engage in this exercise of gratitude, so in turn, I will embarrass the following people who helped shape this book and the ideas in it, in ways big and small:

Brittany, you know all my secrets and never judge. Thank you for teaching me the real meaning of joy. Mercedes, thank you for being such a rock-solid human being, consistent and kind. Oh, and for bringing Ryan and Judd into my life, because they really light up my world. RJS, you are magic. Pure magic. Camilla, I wake up every day and try to live as well as you and love my people as hard as you love your people. Aiesha, you are my sister. Thank you for being tender with me.

Bobby, Caity, Daria, Goldie, Josie, Lindsey, Phill, Zara: You are the voices I hear in my head all day. Thanks for making me laugh.

Irin, Rebecca: Anything smart I've ever said out loud is something I learned from you. Thanks for teaching me about living with integrity.

Sarah, Jesse, Jocelyn, Brad, Jenni, Richard, Molly, John: Thank you for opening your homes to me and being my steady coast-to-coast dinner dates.

Greta, I keep reading that it's impossible to make meaningful new friends at our age, so thank you for making room in your life for me.

Samin, your generosity knows no bounds. You give so much more than you take and I cannot thank you enough.

Cord, thank you for always picking the right bottle of wine and for having hard conversations with me.

Alexis, you told me I could do this and I foolishly believed you. Thanks for bringing Anthony and Poppy into our family. They're the best.

Shani, how do you properly thank someone who saved you? I don't know but I know that you are my home.

Lastly, Ann. We did it. Of course we did it.

I am overwhelmed, *truly overwhelmed*, by the love of my friends. There are too many of you to name but I will find you and tell you that you mean the world to me. I cannot believe my dumb luck that I get to be alive at the same time as you. I love you all so damn much.

ANN WOULD LIKE TO THANK

Gail Ross, thanks for buying in early (2009!), nudging me for years to give you a book proposal to sell, and being such a fierce advocate when I did. Truly, I am indebted to everyone who has ever edited me and made me the writer I am today: Thanks to *Feministing* original recipe and my *Tomorrow* magazine crew, who taught me the power of collaboration. Thank you Laura Bertocci for the editorial support and Jacque Boltik for your technical brilliance.

Bridget, how can I ever thank you for being my deepest-rooted friend, and for always supporting me without conditions or judgment? Josh, you have always been the bringer of magos—a true light of my life for a quarter century. Lara, I love that we both meant it when we slurred "I commit to YOU." Sarah, your generosity is boundless, and I am in awe of how you are both

Acknowledgments

joyfully spontaneous and rock-solid reliable. Beth, thank you for modeling for me what it means to truly support the communities you care about—I'm honored to be part of yours. CPR, thank you for being forever FSE, and Nikki, thank you for keeping it weird in the best way. Hilda, I am grateful for our conversations in the car idling outside my house. J. Ryan, thank you for inviting me into your community of writers. Tamara, thank you for asking the best questions and always saving me a seat. Jade, I love scheming with you. Kenesha, Stacy, Mercedes, Ryan, Aiesha, Colleen, Jorge, Ben, Amelia, Lauren, George!, Jen, Samhita, Erin, Anna, Jessica, Glynnis, and so many other beloved friends: Thank you for all the walks and meals and perfectly timed texts. Please know that these little things are not little at all. Please know how profoundly you have shaped me.

I am grateful for my family. Mom and Dad, thank you for showing me that nothing worthwhile is easy all the time, for loving me so deeply, for modeling generosity, and for teaching me to work hard to stay close to the people who are important to me.

Will, thank you for being more excited about my work than I am (how is that even possible?), for doing more than your share of the admin, for talking me down and puffing me up, for preheating, for your steadiness in even the most chaotic times. I'm so glad we get to do this together.

Amina, you are core to me. Thank you for every single thing.

I love you all so much.

Notes

PROLOGUE

xiv *You know that clip of Oprah talking about Gayle*: Oprah Winfrey, interview by Barbara Walters, *A Barbara Walters Special: Oprah, the Next Chapter*, aired December 9, 2010, on ABC, https://www.youtube.com/watch?v=Do1rpXCP3Fs.

xv *We had also started a podcast together*: *Call Your Girlfriend*, https://www.callyourgirlfriend.com.

xvii *It's called Shine Theory*: https://www.shinetheory.com.

xvii *everyone from Victoria's Secret to Reese Witherspoon has tried to co-opt it*: Victoria's Secret used it in an Instagram caption on a post selling shiny swimwear, but the post is now deleted after a cease and desist from our lawyer. (Thanks, Quinn!) And the working title of a Reese Witherspoon TV show was *Shine Theory* until we asked for credit and they changed the name. Kacey Musgraves, a guest on the show, said in March

213

2018 that it was "based on the idea that women who support each other I guess shine brighter." (Myles Tanzer, "Kacey Musgraves Knows Love Makes the World Go Round," *The Fader*, March 22, 2018, https://www.thefader.com/2018/03/22 /kacey-mugraves-golden-hour-interview.)

ONE The Spark

1   *OK, actually, it was the prom episode of* Gossip Girl: Technically there have been many prom episodes of this show, but this one aired near the end of season two. *Gossip Girl*, season 2, episode 24, "Valley Girls," directed by Mark Piznarski, written by Josh Schwartz and Stephanie Savage, aired May 11, 2009, on The CW, https://www.imdb.com/title /tt1393347.

4   *i'm excited to meet aminatou sow*: Aminatou Sow's name is pronounced ah-mee-NAH-too soh. Dayo's name is pronounced DIE-oh. And Ann Friedman's name is pronounced an FREED-man, with a seriously nasal "a" sound when you say it in a Northern Midwest accent.

7   *He got his comeuppance many years later, when an entire episode of the radio show* This American Life *was dedicated to his misbehavior*: *This American Life*, episode 640, "Five Women," produced by Chana Joffe-Walt, aired March 2, 2018, https:// www.thisamericanlife.org/640/five-women.

14   *Orszagasm.com*: Sadly it's no longer online, but *The Economist* described it as "a blog site [. . .] devoted to chronicling the affairs of this unlikely Casanova with a calculator, who sported not one but two BlackBerry holsters." "American Politics: Something Rotten," *The Economist*, August 24,

2013, https://www.economist.com/books-and-arts/2013/08/24 /something-rotten.

17 *Emily Langan* is an associate professor of communication at Wheaton College, https://www.wheaton.edu/academics /faculty/emily-langan.

18 *The same combination of emotions can be categorized many ways*: Angela Chen, *Ace: What Asexuality Reveals About Desire, Society, and the Meaning of Sex* (Boston: Beacon Press, 2020). Angela Chen is a senior editor at *MIT Technology Review* and a freelance journalist, http://www.angelachen.org.

TWO Obsessed

22 *"Spring's Must-Have Denim Skirt"*: "Spring's Must-Have Denim Skirt: Time to Sharpen Your Pencils," Refinery29, March 2, 2009, https://www.refinery29.com/en-us/springs-must have-denim-skirt-t.

24 *Some researchers will tell you that men are socialized to be more interested in forming friendships around doing activities together, while for many women activities are less important*: Jacob M. Vigil, "Asymmetries in the Friendship Preferences and Social Styles of Men and Women," *Human Nature* 18 (June 2007): 143–61.

25 *You have probably heard about the 10,000-hour rule*: Malcolm Gladwell, "Complexity and the Ten-Thousand-Hour Rule," *The New Yorker*, August 21, 2013, https://www .newyorker.com/sports/sporting-scene/complexity-and-the -ten-thousand-hour-rule.

25 *The number is based on research done by K. Anders Ericsson*: K. Anders Ericsson, Ralf Th. Krampe, and Clemens

Tesch-Römer, "The Role of Deliberate Practice in the Acquisition of Expert Performance," *Psychological Review* 100, no. 3 (1993): 363–406.

25 *who has said — twist! — that Gladwell misinterpreted his work*: *The Learning Leader Show*, episode 147, "Anders Ericsson — What Malcolm Gladwell Got Wrong About the 10,000 Hour Rule," hosted by Ryan Hawk, aired August 3, 2016, https://learningleader.com/episode-147-anders-ericsson.

25 *Jeffrey A. Hall, a researcher at the University of Kansas who has avoided being summarized by Gladwell, actually timed the early stages of friendships*: Jeffrey Hall, "How Many Hours Does It Take to Make a Friend?," *Journal of Social and Personal Relationships* 36, no. 4 (March 2018): 1278–1296.

41 *We were creating our "story of sameness"*: Deborah Tannen, *You're the Only One I Can Tell: Inside the Language of Women's Friendships* (New York: Ballantine Books, 2017).

THREE Chosen Family

45 *In her dissertation on best friendships, communications professor Emily Langan studied whether attachment theory — a way of describing how children bond with their parents — might also apply to platonic intimate relationships*: Emily Langan, "A Friend Like You: Attachment and Maintenance Strategies in Young Adult Friendships" (PhD diss., Arizona State University, 2001).

52 *The use of "chosen family" was first studied by the anthropologist Kath Weston*: Kath Weston, *Families We Choose: Lesbians, Gays, Kinship*, rev. ed. (1991; New York: Columbia University Press, 1997).

52 *for queer people in the late 20th century, the choice to create*

alternative bonds outside of one's biological family was often "borne out of necessity": Brianna Sharpe, " 'Chosen Families' Give LGBTQ Parents and Kids the Support They May Lack," *HuffPost Canada*, November 12, 2018, https://www.huffing tonpost.ca/entry/chosen-families-lgbtq_ca_5cd575e3e4b07 bc729784bee.

54 *"Love was nice if it came afterwards, but it was not considered a good reason for marriage"*: Stephanie Coontz, "Marriage vs. Friendship," August 2, 2019, in *Call Your Girlfriend*, hosted by Aminatou Sow and Ann Friedman, produced by Gina Delvac, podcast, https:// www.callyourgirlfriend .com/episodes/2019/08/02/marriage-vs-friendship. Stephanie Coontz is the director of research and public education for the Council on Contemporary Families and emeritus faculty of history and family studies at the Evergreen State College in Olympia, Washington, https://www.stephaniecoontz.com.

FOUR   I Don't Shine If You Don't Shine

60 *63 percent of women say they've never had a mentor*: Stephanie Neal, Jazmine Boatman, and Linda Miller, *Women As Mentors: Does She or Doesn't She?* (Pittsburgh: DDI, 2013), https://www.ddiworld.com/ddi/media/trend-research/women asmentors_rr_ddi.pdf?ext=.pdf.

60 *"Everyone we spoke with over age 40 could name a mentor in his or her professional life, but younger people often could not"*: Thomas J. DeLong, John J. Gabarro, and Robert J. Lees, "Why Mentoring Matters in a Hypercompetitive World," *Harvard Business Review*, January 2008, https://hbr.org/2008 /01/why-mentoring-matters-in-a-hypercompetitive-world.

61 *after age 35 or so—and certainly if you start having kids— the wage gap really starts yawning open*: Elise Gould, Jessica Schieder, and Kathleen Geier, *What Is the Gender Pay Gap and Is It Real?* (Washington, DC: Economic Policy Institute, October 20, 2016), https://www.epi.org/publication/what-is-the -gender-pay-gap-and-is-it-real.

65 *women are less likely than men to be promoted internally*: Jess Huang et al., *Women in the Workplace 2019* (New York: McKinsey & Company, 2019), https://www.mckinsey.com/fea tured-insights/gender-equality/women-in-the-workplace -2019.

74 *people who are unafraid to share their knowledge and resources with others in their community are the most likely to succeed over the long term*: Adam Grant, *Give and Take: Why Helping Others Drives Our Success* (New York: Penguin Books, 2013).

75 *The* New York Times *called it "the Shalane Effect"*: Lind- say Crouse, "How the 'Shalane Flanagan Effect' Works," *New York Times*, November 11, 2017, https://www.nytimes .com/2017/11/11/opinion/sunday/shalane-flanagan-marathon -running.html.

75 *people prefer to make friends with other people who can help them achieve their goals*: Eric B. Slotter and Wendi L. Gardner, "Can You Help Me Become the 'Me' I Want to Be? The Role of Goal Pursuit in Friendship Formation," *Self and Identity* 10, no. 2 (2011): 231–247.

77 *Natalia Oberti Noguera is the founder and CEO of Pipeline Angels*, http://nataliaobertinoguera.com.

77 *There was a whole Supreme Court case fought about this*: Led- *better v. Goodyear Tire & Rubber Co.*, 550 U.S. 618 (2007).

77 *The first bill that President Obama signed into law was the*

Notes

Lilly Ledbetter Fair Pay Act: Megan Slack, "From the Archives: President Obama Signs the Lilly Ledbetter Fair Pay
Act," *The White House* (blog), January 30, 2012, https://
obamawhitehouse.archives.gov/blog/2012/01/30/archives
-president-obama-signs-lilly-ledbetter-fair-pay-act.

78 *Decades before "me too" became a widespread shorthand*:
The "me too" movement was founded in 2006 by activ-
ist Tarana Burke, who had been using the phrase for years
to give voice to survivors of sexual harassment and assault,
particularly Black women and girls and other young women
of color. "Me too" came into more widespread use in 2017.
"History & Vision," Me Too website, 2018. https://metoo
mvmt.org/about/#history.

78 *Ann used to have an elaborate inside "joke" with a few other
women in media*: The cocreators of "The Island" are Deanna
Zandt, Esther Kaplan, and Tracy Van Slyke.

79 *Alyssa Mastromonaco* is a former advisor to President Barack
Obama, https://speakerhub.com/speaker/alyssa-mastromonaco.

79 *The women on staff also devised a strategy they called "amplification"*: Juliet Eilperin, "How a White House Women's
Office Strategy Went Viral," *Washington Post*, October 25,
2016, https://www.washingtonpost.com/news/powerpost/wp
/2016/10/25/how-a-white-house-womens-office-strategy
-went-viral.

80 *Ann wrote a column that introduced the concept to the world*:
Ann Friedman, "Shine Theory: Why Powerful Women Make
the Greatest Friends," *The Cut*, May 31, 2013, https://www.
thecut.com/2013/05/shine-theory-how-to-stop-female-comp
etition.html.

80 *Shine Theory was getting a lot of traction as a hashtag*: For a

219

taste of the public conversation about Shine Theory, we recommend searching for #ShineTheory on Twitter, Facebook, or Instagram.

82 *Alexandria Ocasio-Cortez, a representative from New York, tweeted*: Alexandria Ocasio-Cortez (@AOC), "I am so incredibly proud of @AyannaPressley," Twitter, December 11, 2018, https://twitter.com/AOC/status/1072690288102137856.

82 *Pressley thanked Ocasio-Cortez for "living #shinetheory out loud"*: Ayanna Pressley (@AyannaPressley), "And I of you. Thank you for living #shinetheory out loud, for sparking a movement, inspiring a generation & leading the charge on a #GreenNewDeal Select Cmte @sunrisemvmt," Twitter, December 11, 2018, https://twitter.com/ayannapressley/status /1072700652319580160?lang=en.

82 *Ilhan Omar, a representative from Minnesota and the first Somali American elected to Congress, has called Ocasio-Cortez her "partner in justice"*: Ilhan Omar (@IhanMN), "with my partner in justice @Ocasio2018 #doubletrouble," Twitter, November 27, 2018, https://twitter.com/IlhanMN /status/1067596311577468930.

82 *In an interview about how this group of new congresswomen had been early in calling for an impeachment inquiry into President Trump, Omar said, "I think he is terrified by any women who are practicing Shine Theory, who have each other's back"*: Full Frontal with Samantha Bee, "Ilhan Omar: Impeachment Pioneer," produced by Razan Ghalayini with Julie Levitsky, aired October 2, 2019, on TBS, https://www.tbs.com/shows/full-frontal-with-samantha-bee /clips/ilhan-omar-impeachment-pioneer.

FIVE The Stretch

83 *you cannot lose a tampon so far up inside your body that it's gone forever*: "Help! I Think I Might Have Lost My Tampon Inside My Vagina," Planned Parenthood website, January 13, 2012, https://www.plannedparenthood.org/learn/teens/ask-experts/help-i-think-i-might-have-lost-my-tampon-inside-my-vagina.

95 *Jordan Pickell* is a registered clinical counselor and trauma therapist in Vancouver, British Columbia, http://jordanpickell counselling.ca.

SIX The Friendweb

100 *We first got to know each other's long-distance friends in the comments on shared Google Reader posts*: Google Reader was active from October 7, 2005, to July 1, 2013. The Google Reader website (https://www.google.com/reader/about) now reads, "We understand you may not agree with this decision, but we hope you'll come to love these alternatives as much as you loved Reader." We did not come to love any of these alternatives.

100 *#SquadGoals, an aspirational concept for how you'd like your crew of friends to be perceived, came into popular use courtesy of Taylor Swift*: A Google search for "Taylor Swift + squad" yields lots of iconic images, as well as charts on who's in and who's out: https://www.vulture.com/2019/08/taylor-swift-squad-timeline-katy-perry-karlie-kloss.html.

102 *Within a few years, even Swift was critical of squads*: Taylor Swift, "30 Things I Learned Before Turning 30," *Elle*, March

6, 2019, https://www.elle.com/culture/celebrities/a26628467
/taylor-swift-30th-birthday-lessons.

102 *Some black widows' webs are so elastic that you can pluck the
threads like guitar strings*: Science News Staff, "Black Widows Spin Super Silk," *Science*, December 31, 1996, https://
www.sciencemag.org/news/1996/12/black-widows-spin-super
-silk.

103 *Some spider silk outperforms Kevlar by 300 percent*: Ingi
Agnarsson, Matjaž Kuntner, and Todd A. Blackledge, "Bio-
prospecting Finds the Toughest Biological Material: Extraor-
dinary Silk from a Giant Riverine Orb Spider," *PLoS ONE* 5,
no. 9 (September 16, 2010): e11234.

103 *"Each individual is considered a node in a larger network"*:
Lydia Denworth, *Friendship: The Evolution, Biology, and Ex-
traordinary Power of Life's Fundamental Bond* (New York:
W. W. Norton & Company, 2020).

103 *what appears to be the very first map of social networks*: Denworth, *Friendship*.

104 *In 2013, the Massachusetts Institute of Technology's Media
Lab created a tool*: Immersion website, MIT Media Lab, 2013,
https://immersion.media.mit.edu (the Immersion project is no
longer active).

105 *Dunbar's number*: Robin Ian MacDonald Dunbar, "Coevo-
lution of Neocortical Size, Group Size and Language in Humans," *Behavioral and Brain Sciences* 16, no. 4 (December
1993): 681–735.

106 *William K. Rawlins* is Stocker Professor of Interpersonal
Communication in the School of Communication Studies at
Ohio University, http:/www.ohiocommstudies.com/people
/rawlins.

106 *there is little to no research concerning dynamics within friend groups*: In an email sent February 2, 2020, Rawlins confirmed that there is precious little written on the subject of friendship groups and it is a topic that he has never addressed either.

SEVEN The Trapdoor

118 *the trapdoor of racism*: Wesley Morris, "Dumber Than Your Average Bear," *Grantland*, June 24, 2015, https://grantland .com/features/dumber-than-your-average-bear. Wesley Morris is a critic-at-large for the *New York Times*, https://www .nytimes.com/by/wesley-morris.

122 *Get Out* is a 2017 film written and directed by Jordan Peele about a black man who goes home with his white girlfriend to meet her family. SPOILER: He discovers that her family is hypnotizing and lobotomizing black people—who are in "the Sunken Place."

125 *"broken windows" theory*: George L. Kelling and James Q. Wilson, "Broken Windows," *The Atlantic*, March 1982. Wilson and Kelling used broken windows as a metaphor for disorder within neighborhoods. They argued that if a window is broken and not repaired, soon all the windows in the building will be broken.

128 *Her hometown was about 98 percent white*: Isabel Wilkerson, "Seeking a Racial Mix, Dubuque Finds Tension," *New York Times*, November 3, 1991. Dubuque is described as a "virtually all-white city of 58,000 people. . . . [A] tradition-bound, heartland city of mostly Irish and German Catholics, where racial minorities make up 2 percent of the population and where there are only 331 black residents scattered across the city."

129 *42 percent of death sentences are handed to Black Americans*: "NAACP Death Penalty Fact Sheet," NAACP website, January 17, 2017, https://www.naacp.org/latest/naacp-death -penalty-fact-sheet.

130 *This hateful stereotype dates back to 19th-century minstrel shows*: Blair L. M. Kelley, "Here's Some History Behind That 'Angry Black Woman' Riff the NY Times Tossed Around," *The Root*, September 25, 2014, https://www.the root.com/here-s-some-history-behind-that-angry-black -woman-rif-1790877149.

131 *Being labeled as angry ensures that Black women are not allowed to experience a full range of emotions*: Brittney Cooper, *Eloquent Rage: A Black Feminist Discovers Her Superpower* (New York: St. Martin's Press, 2018).

131 *Brittney Cooper, historian and author of* Eloquent Rage: A Black Feminist Discovers Her Superpower, *told NPR*: Mayowa Aina, "Harnessing the Power of 'The Angry Black Woman,'" *All Things Considered*, NPR, February 24, 2019, https://www.npr.org/2019/02/24/689925868/harnessing-the -power-of-the-angry-black-woman.

132 *Pat Parker's poem*: Pat Parker, "For the white person who wants to know how to be my friend," *Movement in Black* (Ithaca, NY: Firebrand Books, 1978), https://lithub.com/three -poems-by-pat-parker.

133 *Ann wrote the article explaining Shine Theory*: Friedman, "Shine Theory," *The Cut*.

134 *"the total complex of relations between people living in society"*: *Merriam-Webster*, s.v. "politics," https://www.merriam -webster.com/dictionary/politics.

134 *"Both white and black Americans prove to be more optimistic*

Notes

than accurate in their descriptions of their personal race relations": Kathleen Korgen, *Crossing the Racial Divide: Close Friendships Between Black and White Americans* (Westport, CT: Praeger, 2002).

134 *42 percent of white people said they had close friends of another race*: Tom W. Smith, *Measuring Inter-racial Friendships: Experimental Comparisons* (Chicago: National Opinion Research Center, University of Chicago, 1999).

135 *To say that Berry's results were eye-opening would be an understatement*: Brent Berry, "Friends for Better or for Worse: Interracial Friendship in the United States as Seen through Wedding Party Photos," *Demography* 43, no. 3 (August 2006): 491–510

135 *Researchers have found that Black children segregate as a self-protective measure*: Cinzia Pica-Smith, "Ask Code Switch: What About Your Friends," January 22, 2020, on *Code Switch*, hosted by Shereen Marisol Meraji and Gene Demby, podcast, https://www.npr.org/transcripts/798367810. Cinzia Pica-Smith is an associate professor of Human Services & Rehabilitation Studies at Assumption College.

136 *Toni Morrison summed up the true function of racism*: Toni Morrison, "Black Studies Center public dialogue. Pt. 2," Portland State University, Special Collections: Oregon Public Speakers, May 30, 1975, https://pdxscholar.library.pdx.edu/orspeakers/90.

137 *"Freedom is like taking a bath. You got to keep doing it every day"*: Suzanne Braun Levine and Mary Thom, eds., *Bella Abzug: How One Tough Broad from the Bronx Fought Jim Crow and Joe McCarthy, Pissed Off Jimmy Carter, Battled for the Rights of Women and Workers, Rallied Against War and*

for the Planet, and Shook Up Politics Along the Way (New York: Farrar, Straus and Giroux, 2008), 124. Flo Kennedy was known for her one-liners.

138   *Researchers have found that interracial relationships tend to end sooner than same-race relationships if it's the* only *interracial relationship for one or both parties*: Ray Reagans, "Differences in Social Difference: Examining Third Party Effects on Relational Stability," *Social Networks* 20, no. 2 (April 1998): 143–57.

138   *this discomfort is also a "potential door"*: Robin DiAngelo, "White Fragility," August 31, 2018, in *Call Your Girlfriend*, hosted by Ann Friedman and Aminatou Sow, produced by Gina Delvac, podcast, https://www.callyourgirlfriend.com /episodes/2018/8/31/white-fragility. Robin DiAngelo is Affiliate Associate Professor of Education at the University of Washington, https://robindiangelo.com.

EIGHT   See You on the Internet

141   *It was the most compelling version of our friendship, translated to audio*: *Call Your Girlfriend* episode archive, https://www. callyourgirlfriend.com/episodes.

141   *the frivolous blog we'd started together in the early days of our friendship*: It was called *Instaboner*. LOL. https://insta boner.wordpress.com.

143   Serial *became the first audio megahit*: *Serial* launched in October 2014 and by the end of that year had been downloaded 40 million times. Amy Roberts, "The 'Serial' Podcast: By the Numbers," CNN, December 23, 2014, https://www .cnn.com/2014/12/18/showbiz/feat-serial-podcast-btn/index .html.

145 *The things that many teens are doing with their phones—like texting or sharing selfies—serve the same purpose and encompass the same "core qualities as face-to-face relationships"*: Joanna C. Yau and Stephanie M. Reich, "Are the Qualities of Adolescents' Offline Friendships Present in Digital Interactions?," *Adolescent Research Review* 3 (May 2017): 339–50.

145 *The study's authors speculate that this is because different generations are using different apps, in different ways*: Denworth, *Friendship*.

146 *Aminatou has had her phone set on Do Not Disturb since 2012*: As of publication, Aminatou's phone is no longer on DND. She now lives in the light.

146 *Does social technology draw us closer to our friends or isolate us*: Robert Kraut and Moira Burke, "Internet Use and Psychological Well-Being: Effects of Activity and Audience," *Communications of the ACM* 58, no. 12 (December 2015): 94–100.

149 *there was a trend of people changing their status to "in a relationship" with their platonic bestie*: Katie Notopoulos, "No One Wants to Admit They're in a Relationship on Facebook Anymore," *BuzzFeed*, January 6, 2015, https://www.buzzfeednews.com/article/katienotopoulos/the-demise-of-making-it-facebook-official.

150 *They have, famously, been friends for more than 40 years and call each other four times a day*: Lisa Kogan, "The *O* Interview: Gayle and Oprah, Uncensored," *O, The Oprah Magazine*, August 2006, https://www.oprah.com/omagazine/gayle-king-and-oprah-uncensored-the-o-magazine-interview.

150 *Back in 1976, they both worked at a Baltimore TV station*: McKenzie Jean-Philippe, "How Oprah and Gayle's Near

Notes

40-Year Friendship Began—and Why Its Lasted," *O, The Oprah Magazine*, May 23, 2019, https://www.oprahmag.com /life/relationships-love/a26965035/oprah-and-gayle-friendship.

150 *Oprah let her borrow a pair of underwear:* "Gayle King: 'The Night I Wore Oprah's Underwear,'" FORA.tv, YouTube, June 30, 2011, https://www.youtube.com/watch?v=jGs__gV zkeA.

150 *"We were two black girls who loved being black"*: Amy Chozick, "Gayle King Has the Spotlight All to Herself," *New York Times*, October 31, 2018, https://www.nytimes.com/2018/10/31 /business/media/gayle-king-has-the-spotlight-all-to-herself. html.

150 *there is video evidence of them getting cranky and annoyed after too many hours in the car together*: The Oprah Winfrey Show, season 21, episodes 1, 7, 12, 17, 22, "Oprah and Gayle's Big Adventure," originally aired between September 18, 2006, and October 17, 2006, https://www.tvguide.com/tvshows/the -oprah-winfrey-show/episode-5802257/100340.

158 *"On social-networking sites such as Facebook, we think we will be presenting ourselves, but our profile ends up as somebody else—often the fantasy of who we want to be. Distinctions blur"*: Sherry Turkle, *Alone Together: Why We Expect More from Technology and Less from Each Other* (New York: Basic Books, 2012).

161 *"The problem," Karen North, a communications professor at USC Annenberg, told the* New York Post: Gabriela Barkho, "Nobody Has Real Friends Anymore," *New York Post*, November 17, 2016, https://nypost.com/2016/11/17/social-media -is-making-you-a-bad-friend.

228

NINE Too Big to Fail

164 *researchers surveyed hundreds of adults*: Gerald Mollenhorst, Beate Völker, and Henk Flap, "Social Contexts and Core Discussion Networks: Using a Choice-Constraint Approach to Study Similarity in Intimate Relationships," *Social Forces* 86, no. 3 (March 2008): 937–965.

165 *"Even if a cutoff can be traced to a single moment—a cruel thing said or outrageous thing done—that supremely tellable violation usually is the climax to frustrations and disappointments that had been building over time."*: Tannen, *You're the Only One I Can Tell*.

174 *Miriam Kirmayer* is a clinical psychologist and friendship expert, https://www.miriamkirmayer.com.

176 *Kayleen Schaefer* is the author of *Text Me When You Get Home: The Evolution and Triumph of Modern Female Friendships* (New York: Dutton, 2018).

178 *An extremely chipper wikiHow entry*: Adam Dorsay, "How to Save a Friendship," wikiHow website, November 18, 2019, https://www.wikihow.com/Save-a-Friendship.

180 *"Increasingly in Silicon Valley, business partners are looking for help before things go downhill—they're signing up for couples counseling"*: April Dembosky, "Couples Counseling Catches On With Tech Co-Founders," *All Things Considered*, NPR, April 23, 2015, https://www.npr.org/sections/health-shots/2015/04/23/401720041/couples-counseling-catches-on-with-tech-co-founders.

183 *"Success is how high you bounce after you hit bottom—George Patton."*: This is what was written on the sign in our therapist's

Notes

parking garage, but the accurate quote is "Success is how high you bounce when you hit bottom."

TEN The Long Haul

187 *The experts say that, when it comes to friendship, ages 30 to 50 tend to be a low point*: Kunal Bhattacharya et al., "Sex Differences in Social Focus Across the Life Cycle in Humans," *Royal Society Open Science* 3, no. 4 (April 2016).

188 *In a* New Yorker *essay published the year we met, the humorist David Sedaris wrote about the "four burners" theory of life priorities*: David Sedaris, "Laugh, Kookaburra," *The New Yorker*, August 17, 2009, https://www.newyorker.com /magazine/2009/08/24/laugh-kookaburra.

189 *"During my years caring for patients, the most common pathology I saw was not heart disease or diabetes; it was loneliness"*: Vivek Murthy, "Work and the Loneliness Epidemic," *Harvard Business Review*, September 27, 2017, https://hbr .org/cover-story/2017/09/work-and-the-loneliness-epidemic.

189 *In 2018, the UK government appointed a minister to address loneliness*: Ceylan Yeginsu, "U.K. Appoints a Minister for Loneliness," *New York Times*, January 17, 2018, https:// www.nytimes.com/2018/01/17/world/europe/uk-britain-lone liness.html.

189 *and Australians called on their leaders to do the same*: Calla Wahlquist, "'Loneliness Minister' Proposed to Tackle Australian Social Isolation," *The Guardian*, October 18, 2018, https://www.theguardian.com/society/2018/oct/19/loneliness -minister-proposed-to-tackle-australian-social-isolation.

189 *"the distress people feel when reality fails to meet their ideal*

of social relationships": Amy Ellis Nutt, "Loneliness Grows from Individual Ache to Public Health Hazard," *Washington Post*, January 31, 2016, https://www.washingtonpost.com/national/health-science/loneliness-grows-from-individual-ache-to-public-health-hazard/2016/01/31/cf246c56-ba20-11e5-99f3-184bc379b12d_story.html.

189 *The researcher William K. Rawlins puts friendships in three categories*: W. K. Rawlins, "Being There and Growing Apart: Sustaining Friendships During Adulthood." In D. J. Canary and L. Stafford (eds.), *Communication and Relational Maintenance* (San Diego: Academic Press, 1994), 275–94.

198 *Friendships become more important as people age*: William J. Chopik, "Associations among Relational Values, Support, Health, and Well-Being across the Adult Lifespan," *Personal Relationships* 24, no. 2 (April 2017): 408–22.

198 *"I went into the research sort of agnostic to the role of friendship"*: Amanda MacMillan, "Why Friends May Be More Important Than Family," *Time*, June 7, 2017, https://time.com/4809325/friends-friendship-health-family.

199 *Bronnie Ware, an Australian nurse who spent several years caring for patients in the last 12 weeks of their lives, recorded their dying epiphanies and published a book about it*: Bronnie Ware, *The Top Five Regrets of the Dying: A Life Transformed by the Dearly Departing* (2011; repr., London: Hay House, 2012).

199 *"When the universe gives you a crash course in vulnerability, you will discover how crucial and life-preserving good friendship is," the psychologist Harriet Lerner told the* New York Times: Mary Duenwald, "Some Friends, Indeed, Do More Harm Than Good," *New York Times*, September 10, 2002,

https://www.nytimes.com/2002/09/10/health/some-friends -indeed-do-more-harm-than-good.html.

199 *Lerner is the author of* The Dance of Connection: Harriet Lerner, *The Dance of Connection: How to Talk to Someone When You're Mad, Hurt, Scared, Frustrated, Insulted, Betrayed, or Desperate* (2001; repr., New York: William Morrow Paperbacks, 2002).

201 *In one study, participants were asked to assess how steep a hill was*: Simone Schnall et al., "Social Support and the Perception of Geographical Slant," *Journal of Experimental Social Psychology* 44, no. 5 (September 2008): 1246–55.

202 *According to Aristotle, friends hold a mirror up to each other*: Aristotle, *The Nicomachean Ethics*, ed. Lesley Brown, trans. David Ross, rev. ed. (Oxford: Oxford University Press, 2009).

About the Authors

AMINATOU SOW is a writer, interviewer, and cultural commentator who facilitates conversations around the most important issues of our time. She is a frequent public speaker whose talks and interviews lead to candid conversations about ambition, money, and power. Aminatou lives in Brooklyn. **www.aminatou.com / @aminatou**

ANN FRIEDMAN is a journalist, essayist, and media entrepreneur who loves talking to strangers and finding new ways to explain the world. She is a contributing editor to *The Gentlewoman*. Every Friday, she sends a popular email newsletter. Ann lives in Los Angeles. **www.annfriedman.com / @annfriedman**

Together, Aminatou and Ann have hosted the popular podcast *Call Your Girlfriend* since 2014. Every week, they call each other—and, often, a special guest—to discuss work, politics, activism, feminism, health, pop culture, and, of course, friendship. The show is produced by the inimitable Gina Delvac. **www.callyourgirlfriend.com / @callyrgf**

Aminatou and Ann also coined the term Shine Theory together, and have been thrilled to watch it become part of the lexicon as a shorthand for the power of prioritizing collaboration over competition. **www.shinetheory.com**

Big Friendship is both Aminatou and Ann's first book. **www.bigfriendship.com / @bigfriendshipbook**

BIG
FRIENDSHIP

AMINATOU SOW
ANN FRIEDMAN

This reading group guide for Big Friendship *includes an intro-
duction, discussion questions, a conversation with the authors, and
ideas for enhancing your book club. The suggested questions are
intended to help your reading group find new and interesting an-
gles and topics for your discussion. We hope that these ideas will
enrich your conversation and increase your enjoyment of the book*

Introduction

A close friendship is one of the most influential and important relationships a human life can contain. Anyone will tell you that! But for all the rosy sentiments surrounding friendship, most people don't talk much about what it really takes to stay close for the long haul.

Now two friends, Aminatou Sow and Ann Friedman, tell the story of their equally messy and life-affirming Big Friendship in this honest and hilarious book that chronicles their first decade in one another's lives. As the hosts of the hit podcast *Call Your Girlfriend*, they've become known for frank and intimate conversations. In this book, they bring that energy to their own friendship—its joys *and* its pitfalls.

Aminatou and Ann define Big Friendship as a strong, significant bond that transcends life phases, geographical locations, and emotional shifts. And they should know: the two have had moments of charmed bliss and deep frustration, of profound connection and gut-wrenching alienation. They have weathered life-threatening health scares, getting fired from their dream jobs, and one unfortunate Thanksgiving dinner eaten in a car in a parking lot in Rancho Cucamonga. Through interviews with friends and experts, they have come to understand that their struggles are not unique. And that the most important part of a Big Friendship is making the decision to invest in one another again and again.

An inspiring and entertaining testament to the power of society's most underappreciated relationship, *Big Friendship* will invite you to think about how your own bonds are formed, challenged, and preserved. It is a call to value your friendships in all of their complexity. Actively choose them. And, sometimes, fight for them.

Topics & Questions for Discussion

1. In the prologue, Sow and Friedman are in a spa trying to repair their friendship. "We were not a romantic couple or estranged family members, but the stakes were just as high for us" (page xiv). Discuss this statement. In your experience, is it true that the stakes for friendship are just as high as romantic or familial relationships? Why or why not?

2. How does the use of "we" inform your reading experience?

3. The authors create a language for understanding friendships, such as social initiators (people whose love language is making and keeping plans) and stretching. Do you see these

concepts at play in your friendships? If not, have you made an effort to recognize and enact these behaviors?

4. How do the authors meld research into their memoir? What effect does this have on your reading experience?

5. Pop culture appears throughout the book contextualizing their friendship as it develops. Sow and Friedman watch Beyoncé in *Obsessed,* listen to Coldplay's *Don't Panic,* and wear T-shirts commemorating "the brattiest teen couple" on *Gossip Girl,* Chuck and Blair. What are some shared pop-culture reference points in your friendships?

6. Sow and Friedman have drastically different upbringings. How do their differences manifest in their relationship and in what ways do these differences allow their friendship to thrive?

7. Shine Theory is defined "as an investment, over the long term, in helping a friend be their best—and relying on their help in return" (page 70). It's one of the many revolutionary concepts in the book to expand the definition of friendship. Is Shine Theory operating in your friendships? If not, what steps can you take to make sure it does?

8. Chosen family is a term used by the LGBTQ community to describe intimate relationships that are freely selected. What does it mean that Sow and Friedman describe each other that way? What is the political importance of this?

9. How is the friendweb different from #SquadGoals? How does the Desert Ladies trip strain Sow and Friedmans' friendweb? What is the solution to the strain?

10. When Sow attends a birthday party of one of Friedman's friends, she's disheartened to find that she's the only Black person in the gathering. What is the significance of this event? How does this demonstrate the trapdoor of racism, an experience articulated by Wesley Morris, as the risk people of color take when they are friends with white people who can disappoint with a "slip of the tongue, or at a campus party, or in a legislative campaign" (page 118). How does this moment highlight an unbridgeable gap between Sow and Friedman?

11. Sow and Friedman share a low moment in their friendship when they retreat into their own corners, despite sharing "an LLC, a bank account, and a trademark" (page 163). How does the breakdown occur? Has this happened in your own friendship before?

12. In couples therapy, Sow and Friedman repair their friendship by "undoing our powerful story of sameness" (page 184). What does this mean?

13. Sow and Friedman emphasize, "active friendships require active maintenance" (page 192). Do you actively invest in your friendships? What does this look like?

14. Now that you've read the book, define Big Friendship. What does it mean to you? And how can you keep it?

A Conversation with Aminatou Sow and Ann Friedman

Congratulations on the success of *Big Friendship*! Did you always know you wanted to write a book together?

We did not! Every single one of our professional collaborations has grown out of our friendship. It's true that we have been obsessed with each other's brains since the moment we first met, but we never once sat down to make a longterm plan for things we would like to make together. At some point, many years deep into our friendship and after many ups and downs, we realized that we had never read a book that captured a relationship like ours. It was then that we started to think, "Well, maybe we should be the ones to write it. And write it together."

What was the cowriting process like? Were you ever surprised by how the other person remembered certain stories? If so, how did you bridge those gaps?

This is both of our first time writing a book so we really went into it with no expectations or experience. We essentially had writing retreats where we could physically be in the same space for weeks at a time. Our process involved really long discussions about each chapter outline before sitting down to write. You won't be surprised to hear that even when we were writing about the same event or a shared experience, we usually had differing perspectives on what had happened or how it had impacted us. It was great when we agreed but when we had diverging experiences, it was actually an opportunity to learn more about how the other person felt. We got to go over our *entire* friendship with a fine tooth comb and that's an experience we probably won't have in any other relationship.

The book begins at a spa where you both try to fix your friendship. It's clear from the start that the stakes are high. What was it like writing and sharing those vulnerable moments in your friendship?

All of the difficult moments you read about in the book are things we both feel resolved about now. If it's in the book, you can be sure that we've talked about it with each other, we've processed it with our therapist(s), and we've done *so much* reflecting on it individually. Our writing process involved a lot of discussions about boundaries, and together we decided which details were necessary to the story and which were too raw or personal to include. Like most things in life, writing the vulnerable parts was easier to do side-by-side with a friend.

A theme that emerges in the book is that it's political to take friendships seriously. Did you always understand and frame friendships this way? Or is this something that came out of writing this book?

Friendship as a site of politics is a concept that we each understood before we met each other and it was vitally important in our other big friendships. We never explicitly discussed it in the early days but it's definitely a huge part of why we became such close friends.

There's a painful incident recounted in the book where Aminatou is disappointed to see that she's the only Black person in a birthday party hosted in Ann's home. It's a profound chapter for its honesty and insight. What did you hope readers would learn from you sharing this incident?

On the simplest level, and we hoped that putting some of our experiences into words would lead to more conversations about interracial friendship. We're hungry for more stories! We wanted to get into the sticky details of how the costs and benefits of interracial friendship are very different for each of us as a Black woman and a white woman, and prompt our readers to examine the nuances of privilege within their own friendships. Then our book happened to come out at a time when a lot of white people were newly engaging with the way racism has a maddening tendency to creep into all of our relationships. We hoped to remind readers that this is not a new phenomenon. That all friendships (yes, even friendships between two people of the same race) are affected by the fact that we live in a world that has been shaped by and built on racism, so it does not behoove us to ignore this fact.

And that it's possible to stay connected and be accountable to a friend of a different race.

There are many useful and original concepts in the book like friendweb, Shine Theory, and stretching. How did you conceive and name these concepts?

Almost all friend groups have their own vocabulary and the friendweb was something that ours said for as long as we could remember. Shine Theory was coined when Ann wrote a magazine article about the way we mutually affirmed each other over the years and stretching is a concept we came up when we were writing the book. We are definitely word nerds.

The book describes both of your career trajectories, the hardships, and innovative support networks, such as friendwebs, you utilized to advance. A part of this conversation is that you reveal your salaries. How important was it to you to share your professional journeys with readers?

This sounds very moral high ground, but we really do try to practice what we preach! We wrote about the radical power of transparency in our chapter on Shine Theory, so we wanted to practice that transparency throughout the book. We think this would be a more equitable world if everyone were open about their professional path, their support networks, and, yes, their salary numbers.

Big Friendship points out that there is a lack of resources when it comes to friendships, despite it being one of life's most important intimate relationships. This book feels like a corrective to

this problem. Did you always intend that the book be read that way?

On the hardest days when our friendship was falling apart we both longed for a resource we could turn to and found nothing that addressed our specific problem: how do two real humans, not fictional characters (there is excellent friendship fiction), fix a broken friendship? We're not experts so this isn't self-help. We wanted to share our own story of failing and trying and finally getting it right. This was an invitation to readers who could see the contours of their own friendships in our experience. Our hope was that it would open up a conversation about the importance of friendship in a world that doesn't give it its right due. Our experience isn't universal or unique so we are dying to read books about all kinds of friendships. *Big Friendship* is our tiny contribution to a body of work we are deeply invested in.

What have you been listening to, watching, or reading that readers should take note of?

We are big fans of Mia Birdsong's book *How We Show Up: Reclaiming Family, Friendship and Community*. In some ways it feels like a companion to our book, and it's full of inspiring examples of people who are rejecting the status quo to find their own meaningful ways of being in community with each other. We also devoured season four of *Insecure*, which depicts Issa and Molly going through a rough patch in their big friendship. It resonated *so* deeply with our own experience of being estranged from each other, and it was incredible to see some of those dynamics depicted on screen.

What do you ultimately hope readers will take away from the book?

That friendship can be the main course and not the dessert of life. That it is worth shouting from the rooftops about. That friendship is hard work but it is also rewarding work that enriches your life and teaches you about yourself and how to be in the world.

Enhance Your Book Club

1. Sow and Friedman share their magical origin story: a *Gossip Girl* watch party. Recount your origin story with your friend!

2. Shine Theory is a mutual, meaningful long-term investment. With your group, brainstorm ways to practice Shine Theory. Discuss how and who you can share resources, contacts, and opportunities with.

3. At the beginning of the book, Sow and Friedman go to couples therapy. What are other creative strategies for friendship repair?